M000114284

INSPIRATIONS FROM FELT

By Anthony B. Feltus

Copyright © 2019 by Anthony B. Feltus

All rights reserved. This book or any portion thereof may not be reproduced or used in any manner whatsoever without the express written permission of the publisher except for the use of brief quotations in a book review.

Limits of Liability and Disclaimer of Warranty

The author and publisher shall not be liable for your misuse of this material. This book is strictly for informational and educational purposes. The purpose of this book is to educate and entertain. The author and/or publisher do not guarantee that anyone following these techniques, suggestions, tips, ideas, or strategies will become successful. The author and/or publisher shall have neither liability nor responsibility to anyone with respect to any loss or damage caused, or alleged to be caused, directly or indirectly by the information contained in this book.

Views expressed in this publication do not necessarily reflect the views of the publisher.

Printed in the United States of America

ISBN: 9781092406116

Dedication

This book is dedicated to my mother Deborah Cobb. I was holding her hand as she took her last breath, I whispered in her ear; be patient with me God is not who through with me yet.

To my father James H. Feltus, who showed me it is not how you start, but more how you finish.

My siblings; Marcella, Bernetha, Jason, and James II, I wouldn't trade them for anything.

My children; Britini and Seth, you are by far my greatest accomplishment, and also to my three granddaughters; Brionna, Taylor, and Arianna.

My two nieces; Tiffany and Amber, and nephews; Jules, Julien, and Damien.

To my three ex-wives, thank you for enduring so much of me.
Finally, to everyone else that sowed into me or allowed me to sow into them.

Thank You All, To God Be the Glory!

Anthony

FAITHFUL

I don't write these inspirations as someone who has arrived or nearly has it all together. But more of someone who has decided through faith, to commit to something. Faithful implies long-continued and steadfast fidelity to whatever one is bound to by a pledge, duty, or obligation. Being Faithful has its reward with God and man. Abraham of the Bible was considered a righteous man because of his faith. David, also a biblical character, through faith, was said to be a man after God's heart. Not that he had a heart like God, but he faithfully sought the heart of God. I don't believe that God is so much concerned with how many degrees you have or how much money you have, not even how talented you are, but having faith and being Faithful will move God like nothing else. Let's just be, you probably won't be Faithful to everything, but being Faithful to God will set everything else straight.

Be Inspired!

DECISIONS & CHOICES

After attending a star-filled event I realized that we looked similar, we dressed similar, and for the most part, we acted similarly. So, I asked myself what was the difference between them and me. What I came up with were Decisions and Choices. When I went left maybe I should have gone right, when I said yes, I should have said no. Decisions and Choices, our lives hang in the balance every second based on the two. Where you live, work, eat, who you spend time with, and even where you worship. There is a biblical passage found in Proverbs 3:5-6. It says, Bruh, put your trust in the Most High with all your heart. Stop tripping; don't be acting like you know it all. Look to God in all you do, and He will show you which path to take Decisions and Choice.

Be Inspired!

COMPETITIVENESS

I have come to believe that one of the greatest challenges we face, if not the greatest, is competitiveness. Now I know pride won't let us openly admit that we are in competition, but if we examine our actions clearly, we are competing to an end of frustration and despair. From the little child on the playground, the mother who wants her child to look the best when they leave the house, best hair weave, the preacher preparing his sermon, the woman looking for that dress or pair of shoes, the athlete, sexual performance, the doctor, the lawyer, the scientists, the cake baker, weight loss, the largest church, the "phatest" ride, even the janitor says I'm going to be the best janitor. The reason we are always competing is we are always comparing and the reason we are comparing is this society encourages competition. Competition by definition, which is from Latin origin, says that you are striving, and you have an adversary. Are we in competition against the wrong thing or person? There is a biblical passage found in 1 Peter 5:8 that says be serious, "Be alert, your adversary, your enemy, your opponent, the devil, is walking around like a roaring lion trying to trip you up." Since your soul is more important than your prestige, pick your battles and your weapons carefully and finally my friends,

Be Inspired!

MERRY CHRISTMAS EVERYDAY

It does not matter what time of year you are reading this, the very thought that Jesus was born, died, and rose again with ALL POWER, makes it Christmas Day. Just think about it, it is a day of good food, good fun, and good fellowship, but also a day of remembrance. Now I don't know exactly what day Jesus was born, frankly, at this point in my life, the date of His birth is not a factor, the fact that He was born, and the purpose of His birth is the most important thing to me. My friends and I celebrate more frequently than December 25th. The whole theme of Christmas should be love. But I also like the word Intervention, it is defined as an occasion on which a person with a behavioral problem is confronted by someone that really cares about them in an attempt to persuade them to address their issues. Now you do the math, Love + Intervention = Jesus. There is a biblical passage found in John 3:16 that say, "For God so loved the world that He gave His only begotten Son". So, when you are looking at your gifts this Christmas remember to look at the gift God gave you!

Be Inspired!

COMPLETING

The holidays have come and gone. Now it's a new year. Many have already made and failed at new resolutions. Some folk decided not to even make new resolutions, I'm in that number. I said to myself, self, why would you make new resolutions when you already have unkept ones from so many years. Everyone is talking about this is the season for this and the season for that. I say it's time for us to finish some unfinished stuff vs. continuing in the same perpetual cycle of starting and not completing anything. A good or great idea is nothing more than that if it's not seen through to completion. Some definitions of finishing are, bring to an end, complete, accomplish, fulfill. Rather than spending this entire year frustrated from not finishing, seek to reap the reward of finishing. There is a biblical passage found in Ecclesiastes 7:8 it says, "The end of a thing is better than its beginning. To finish one thing is better than starting ten."

Be Inspired!

AMAZING GRACE

A fellow by the name of John Newton pinned these lyrics "Through many dangerous toils and snares I've already come", many years ago. They are from the song, Amazing Grace. Now, it's one thing to join in and sing this song in your Sunday service. But to know from real life experiences God's Amazing Grace is another thing. You see Grace says no matter what you/I did we couldn't earn it (Grace) because it's God's unmerited favor. When we slow down enough to look back over our lives, (daily inventory), we can see the Grace of God all over our lives. From the job we didn't qualify for but got, the near misses on the freeway, the A in class when we did C work, the good report on the medical exam, the house when the credit score said no, and freedom from some long or short term bondage we were wrapped up in, or when you thought you were going to lose your mind. All this was a result of God's Grace. There is a biblical passage found in Luke 17:15 that says, "One of the 10 realizing he had been healed came back to God and gave Him Crazy Praise. God was like man you know what you are grateful and you're not even one of mine". While everyone is putting on the finishing touches for this Christmas event, take a second to say, "Lord, I thank you!"

Be Inspired!

MY MOTHER DEBORAH COBB

MULLIGANS

I'm not a golfer at all but I heard a term associated with it that was interesting; Mulligan. A mulligan is a second chance to perform an action, usually, after the first chance went wrong through bad luck or a blunder. I said to myself, "How many Mulligans have I been given?" It says through bad luck, which says it might not have even been my fault. Then it says a blunder, which says I messed up. The definition goes on to say that the player gets another play even though it's against the formal rules. The blunder doesn't even count against you on the scorecard. So, the only person that remembers it is the player himself cause there's no record of it. There is a biblical passage found in Psalms 103: 11-12 that says, "As high as the heavens are above the earth so does God increase His mercy toward us that are His and as far as the east is from the west, He has removed our sins (blunders) from us". Thank God for another Mulligan.

Be Inspired!

REASONABLE SERVICE

Having a voice is a great gift, but it also comes with great responsibility. It also has accountability, and dependability attached to it. When asked, "Why I write an inspirational post every Sunday?" I replied, because it is my reasonable service because of what I've been given, and that is a voice. Point is we have all been given some type of gift. The question is, "Do we use it to serve others?" There is a well-known biblical passage found in Matthew 25:15 which talks about the talents that were given. Further, it talks about what was done with the gifts and the outcome of doing. Share your gift.

Be Inspired!

WALK TALL

Everything is not for everyone, so, when I came out of surgery and went to a rehabilitation facility. One of the first things the therapist said to me was, "When you start walking; walk like you want to walk." Well in my mind I said, "I do want to walk, so I will." Later in my spirit, I heard him say, "Walk like you want to walk", but it sounds different. It said to me, "When you are able to walk it will look a certain way, so start walking now the way you want it to look." Many of us have been cut, scared, wounded, bruised, used, abused, talked about, and self-destructive and worse. But we are in therapy now and the therapist, (God), is saying, "Straighten up, stand tall, walk upright, be strong, be courageous, walk with confidence, and don't be afraid." When you get where you are going that's what you want it to look like. Start practicing now for what you want. You can't get to the game and start shooting 3's if you have only been working on free throws.

Be Inspired!

BALANCE

This word is derived from two Latin words. Bi which means having two and Lanx which means scale pan. These together are often associated with the zodiac sign Libra. Usually, when you see a picture of the two scale pans they are not even, slightly or greatly tilted to either one side or the other. This is because they are out of balance. Balance is defined as an even distribution of weight enabling someone or something to remain upright and steady. How does this pertain to us? Thought you would never ask. We find ourselves constantly on a scale trying to balance out our lives. We are slightly or greatly tilted from one side or the other. We probably deal more in extremes. We sometimes have glimpses of some sense of balance. What is needed is what we refer to as a counterbalance. This is a weight that has the opposite effect to that of another as to prevent disproportion or uneven distribution. There is a familiar biblical passage found in Philippians 4:7 that make reference to balance, but it uses the word Peace. It says to, "Pray and tell God what you need and then thank Him, and you will experience peace."

Be Inspired!

THANKFULNESS

It was a great time to not only be grateful but also to show gratitude. We are all, most times, probably better recipients of gratitude than givers. Jesus himself said, "It is more blessed to give than to receive." Contrary to what some might believe, the word blessed does not mean that you will have more because of your giving it means that you will be happy or favored because you gave. I had an experience this past week where I visited a sick friend at the hospital. I didn't know how sick they were, but they requested that I come and pray for them. Of course, I felt honored and so very humbled but also compelled to go. I went and gave of myself and before I left, we were in agreement that God reigned supreme. I'm saddened to say that my friend passed away the day before Thanksgiving. I wasn't there but I was told that they asked for me before passing. I'm grateful to have been a friend of a friend.

Be Inspired!

RELATIONSHIP

Today's inspiration is about Relationship. The word relationship is defined as the way two or more concepts, objects, or people are connected or the state of being connected. So, by definition, you can't be in a relationship with anything without being connected to it. And you can't be connected to anything without being in a relationship with it. There is a very familiar biblical passage found in Luke 15:11-32 about a young man referred to as the prodigal (a person who is reckless and wasteful with resources) son. He did not respect and appreciate the connection and relationship he had with his father. So, he left the relationship and became disconnected and fell into a bad state, called prodigal. But he came to himself and said hold up wait a minute something isn't right. I got to clean up what I messed up. Imagine being in a relationship with something vital to your existence like oxygen, eating healthy, or just living right, and saying to yourself I think I'll go live like a fool. Same concept as a prodigal. But God. Standing, waiting, knocking, and looking all for you. Ready to restore the Relationship.

Be Inspired!

SINCERITY

There is a biblical passage found in 1 Chronicles 4: 9-10 that gives an account of a man by the name of Jabez. Most people are familiar with this man because of the prayer he prayed referred to as the Prayer of Jabez. If you just read the account or hear people talk about the prayer or listen to the song written about the prayer you might gather that the prayer is about gaining material wealth. After further review, you will find that the account is really about praying first of all to the right source. We sometimes find ourselves looking in all the wrong places. Secondly, its reference is to the sincerity of the prayer. It's like kids playing in a room and the mother hears two loud noises the first noise she hears she ignores because she knows that it's not that serious, the second noise she jumps up frantically and runs into the room to see what's wrong. She instinctively knows the difference and reacts accordingly. God knows when we are sincere. Lastly, it's about commitment. The man vows upon receiving his request to be loyal and show gratitude to God. Under these conditions, God grants Jabez his request. Are your prayer requests being answered?

Be Inspired!

RESTORATION

It is defined as the action of returning something to its original place, condition, or owner. Several things have to take place in the mind of the restorer before restoration can begin. 1.) Is what is to be restored worth restoring. 2.) Who is the restoration for? 3.) What is the cost of the restoration? The person doing the restoring has to be a visionary or have a picture in their mind of what the finished state will look like. It gives them direction, purpose, and a goal. People restore all kinds of things: houses, clothes, furniture, and even cars. Aren't you glad today that you have met someone (God) that is in the business of human restoration? He thought you were worth all the action necessary to restore you back to the original place, condition, and creator. If you have not met Him there is a biblical passage found in Joel 2nd chapter that says if you turn to Him truly with your heart and not with your stuff. He will restore back the years that were taken from you.

Be Inspired

FEAR

I can remember when I was a lot younger standing on the diving board at the deep end of the (Kankakee) pool for the first time. Scared to death wanting to jump but was paralyzed. I also remember getting in trouble at school early in the day. Having to go the whole day at school, and then walk home knowing that the beat down was coming. You talk about being scared, I can remember being in situations where I was afraid to approach people about situations because of possible outcomes. Even before preaching on a Sunday morning nervous to the point of shaking. These are different examples but what they all have in common is they are all forms of fear. I know of a fellowship that has in their literature that there are at least 100 forms of fear that we are driven by. "But", which is a word that usually negates everything before it. There is a biblical passage found in 2Timothy 1:7 which says that the spirit that God gave us does not make us timid, but gives us power, love, and self-control. I always start off by saying From Felt, but this is really for Felt.

Be Inspired!

FAITH

When you pray, it's not so much in what you pray, because many pray a prayer that they have memorized or that they learned from someone else. When you pray you are praying to a God that already knows. So, you can't impress Him with fancy words. It's the fact that you believe in Him enough to pray that moves Him. There is a biblical passage found in Matthew, Mark and, Luke which gives an account of a woman that had been suffering from a condition for a long time. She tried a lot of things to be healed, none of which were a success. Then, somehow her belief system changed. Her FAITH went to another level. She said to herself, "If I can somehow just touch the hem of His garment that will be enough." It wasn't the hem of the garment that healed the woman, it was her belief system (FAITH). It's possible to believe in something so strongly that even God will be moved. How much FAITH do you have/use?

Be Inspired!

INTERNAL AFFAIRS

This is usually referred to as a division of law enforcement. Its function is to investigate law enforcement, but the investigation is done by members of the same body, hence the term Internal. That came to my mind as I was preparing for my day. We find ourselves looking for external answers to internal questions. The one person that you cannot fool is you. Even at times, if you find yourself living some type of lie, you, if no one else knows it's a lie. Truth be told most of us (except the perfect) have lived an untruth at some point. There is a need to do a personal internal investigation as often as possible so that we can get to the internal truths. Ask God to show YOU who YOU are. There is a biblical passage found in James 1:5 it says, "If any of you don't know or need wisdom, ask God, who gives freely without judging you for asking."

Be Inspired!

STILL STANDING

I was speaking with a friend recently about the fact that it's not because I have been this great person, upstanding, moral in every way, politically correct all the time or even Christian-like in all my affairs. It is because I'm still standing. Something else had to be definitely working in my favor. I could have lost my mind, been in an asylum, locked up in a penal institution for life, or even dead in a wormy grave. But I'm still standing, and if you are reading this, so are you! There is a biblical passage found in Psalms 124 that says, "If it had not been for God who was with us, then we wouldn't have made it thus far". Thank God for His many blessings.

Be Inspired!

IT'S NOT ABOUT ME

There is a book that I read entitled, " It's Not About Me" written by Max Lucado. It was an interesting read because it answered some important questions that I had concerning things that make you go hmmm! We all have experienced, are experiencing, or will experience some things in this life that shake the very foundations that we stand on. They challenge our mental strength, our moral standing, integrity level, spiritual standing, levels of love, our ability to forgive, and sometimes even our physical fitness. The inspiration here is that there is a plan for your life and all of the workings of your life down to the smallest, seemingly unimportant detail, are purposely working to implement this plan. God's plan!

Be Inspired!

LEMONS

Life is filled with a variety of events. Some of them so seemingly small that you barely pay them any attention and some of them are so big that they forever alter the course of your life. I suggest that it is not always the event that alters the course of your life, but often times it's your attitude or your response to the event. You've all heard the expressions, "Got lemons, make lemonade, or if at first you don't succeed try and try again, or there's no hill to a climber", which is my favorite. You have to develop an attitude that promotes positivity and results in the desired outcome. The key to all this is YOU. Pick Yourself up, dust Yourself off, and move Yourself ahead.

Be Inspired!

DEFICIT

One of the hardest things in this life is to overcome a deficit. Even worse is to try and overcome a perceived deficit. This usually occurs when an individual or group of individuals begin to compare themselves to someone else or someone else's situation or circumstances. As the saying goes, "the grass looks so much greener on the other side". To spend time looking at the other side says that you have taken the focus off of you and yours and placed less value on you and what you have. The way to overcome this perceived deficit is to trust God. There is a biblical passage found in Psalm 37:3-4 that says, "Trust in God and do what is right and live and prosper. God will give you the desires of your heart." Is my glass half empty or full, or should I just be thankful for having something in my glass?

Be Inspired!

FLOW

It is a word used to describe a person that is completely absorbed (wrapped up, tied up, sewed up, and in the grips of something) in an activity, or what one does. Another way of describing FLOW is the action of moving along in a steady continuous stream. These 2 definitions combined together describe an unstoppable force. It says that you are focused where you are, and you are actively moving forward to achieve the desired outcome. There is a biblical passage found in John 7:38 that says, "If you believe in God out of you shall FLOW rivers of living waters." FLOW!

Be Inspired!

HOPE

We all have unmet desires, dreams, goals, and ambitions. If we give up on them, we will never see them. What is hope? Hope implies little certainty but suggests confidence or assurance in the possibility that what one desires or longs for will happen. When you have hope it says that you have desire and expectation. With these two how can you give up? Push through wherever you are. It might be the so-called wall, it may even be a physical or emotional situation, any type of addiction, whatever it is "keep hope alive"! There is a biblical passage found in Romans 8:24 that says, "Who hopes for what they already have...HOPE!"

Be Inspired!

LIFE & DEATH

There are many sayings to describe how people feel about this topic. " Live and let live", " Life is for the living", " You only live once ", " Live each day like it's your last", " Live, love, and laugh", I'm sure there are many more. My favorite is " Live until you die". The truth of the matter is there is one thing that all living things have in common. I'm glad you asked. That is DEATH. Every living thing is dying, but not all are living. Let's define living. It's defined as currently active, present, useful, animate (give the appearance of movement), thriving, strong, and vigorous are some words used to define living. If you find yourself on the opposite side of more than a few of these words you are probably just dying. There is a biblical passage found in James 4:14 that says, "You don't know what's going to happen tomorrow, you are a mist that is only here for a little while and then you are gone." Today is the first day of the rest of your life, so get busy living.

Be Inspired!

ENDOWMENT

Today's a good day to examine your life. Questions like; Where have I been? What am I doing? What do I know? What do I have? Who do I know? Where am I going? How do I treat my fellow man? Should be at the top of your list? Another important question is "Do you have life insurance? Hence the word ENDOWMENT. An Endowment is a form of life insurance involving payment of a fixed sum to the insured person on a specified date. What does that mean for you and me? It means that we all have a policy and our premium is being paid by the answers to the above questions. Now that you know that your life has value don't mess up your settlement with the wrong answers to these important questions. The Insurer "God " says to you on that date, you violated clause, Matthew 7:23 which clearly states, "Depart from me you workers of lawlessness I never knew you." Read your declaration pages for your policy.

Be Inspired

WHY LIKE THIS?

Most people can understand the training that goes along with making a sports team. We can even get with military training for we see the need for that type of discipline. But when it comes to our own lives, I think probably the biggest question we will face is " WHY LIKE THIS?". There are circumstances, difficulties, problems, sorrows, hurts, tears, letdowns, setbacks, emotional rollercoaster, backstabbing, trickery, and tomfoolery. And I could go on with those signs of living. We find ourselves asking the question WHY LIKE THIS? There is even a biblical passage found in Matthew 26:39 where Jesus says, "Let this cup pass from me." The reason for this question is that we don't understand or can't see the other side. In my own life, I've been faced with more than I can write in this message. I prayed, I cried, I went through bouts of depression, I wanted to give up, and truth be told I even tried to give up. But after enduring and making it to the other side. I now see why I had to go through as I did. You see your story, nor your glory is for you. Someone will specifically need your experience. The answer to the question "WHY LIKE THIS?" Is the Master has need of you! Go through.

Be Inspired!

MYSTERIOUS WAYS

God speaks in ways sometimes that will blow the mind of even the most elect. There is a biblical passage found in 1 Corinthians 1:27 that says, "He chose the foolish things to confound the wise." So, I'm sitting in the parking lot the other day and this lady walks in front of the vehicle. She had obvious issues. My immediate response was, "I know this woman." I didn't know her name and had never seen her a day in my life, but I recognized her character. I said right away, if she comes to my car and asks for anything, I'm going to let her have it. After all, I have the ability to use words in such a way that makes people think, and I've been around the world, and I've been way up, and I've been way down. I was ready for her. She starts in right away with this long drawn out story about being stranded, mother in the hospital, and needing money. When it was time for me to give her the what for, it was like my mouth got stuck I couldn't even make a sound, my mind went blank. I found myself going into my pocket and giving her exactly what she asked for. When she walked away, I said to myself, "What was that?" 30 seconds passed I looked for the woman and she had vanished. I was so humbled by the encounter. Even in your mind be careful about how you entertain folk.

Be Inspired!

MY SON AND GRANDDAUGHTER

THE POSTURE OF WAITING

At one point in my life, I considered myself an athlete. One thing I learned about athletics was that it was more than just participation. There was with every contest or event something called rules. As an athlete, you train and practice with tenacity and perseverance, but you also know that if you don't follow the rules you can be disqualified. What in the world does that have to do with the " The posture of waiting"? I say everything. While you are waiting for the next chapter in your life, while you are waiting to come out of that bad situation, while you are waiting for that healing, while you are waiting on the next move of God. You must train your body, you must train your mind, and you must train your spirit. All the time staying within the guidelines set before you by God. This is done so that you are not disqualified and forfeit your reward. There is a biblical passage found in Isaiah 40:31 that references this, it says, "Everyone can't wait on the Lord but those that do will be rewarded." To wait for, means to stay where one is or to delay action until a particular time or until something else happens.

Be Inspired!

CARPE DIEM

I have found or should I say I am finding that the more inspiration that I give the more I am inspired. My mind is opening and expanding. So, this phrase was dropped in my spirit, " Carpe Diem" it's Latin for " seize the day". So many times, we have a propensity to speed up into the future or do the polar opposite and go back into the past. Not fully or really getting the most out of what's right in front of us. NOW! There is a biblical passage found in Matthew 6:34 that says, "Don't be tripping about what's going to happen tomorrow what's going on right now is enough for you." Say to yourself each morning when you wake, unless you wake up dead, Carpe Diem, " seize the day"!

Be Inspired!

HOW MUCH DIRT DOES IT TAKE?

How much dirt does it take to fill in a hole, how much water does it take to fill a container, and finally how much food do you have to eat before you can say you are full. I believe that the amount of each can actually be measured if only you know the true measurements of each thing that needs to be filled. That's how it is with changing our lives. Can we truly even measure the condition of our lives, the depth, or the height, or the width of our conditions or situations. There is a biblical passage found in Jeremiah 17: 7-10 specifically 9-10 that addresses this very issue. It concludes by saying, "God knows the measurements." To know God is to know you.

Be Inspired!

TODAY

What a wonderful day it is today. This day is not so wonderful because yesterday was so great. Truth is, some of our yesterdays were the worst, with everything that happened. This day is not so wonderful because It came without its own set of challenges. Truth is, today for some, could be better or worse than yesterday, so that's not it either. Today is so wonderful because I'm here, grace and mercy were extended to me yet again. Not because I was so good or right, but because of the love God has for me. What a wonderful day it is! Please join me in praying a special prayer for a young lady named Taylor Mason. 15 years old just diagnosed with leukemia and other challenges. For we know that the prayers of the righteous avail much.

Be Inspired!

I GOT YOU

There is a biblical passage found in Joshua 1:9 that God ask a question. He says, "Boy didn't I already tell you what you are going to need to achieve success?" He says, "Be strong, be courageous, be not afraid, and don't be tripping cause I'm not going anywhere I got you." Hey, right this very moment I'm facing something that is going to present major challenges for me. This is not something that is exclusive to me, we all have challenges. So, this all means that the challenge itself doesn't determine the outcome, it is ME. God didn't ask the man if he could do these things, He commanded him like He is commanding you and me today be strong, be courageous, be not afraid, and don't be tripping. Whatever your challenges are, we're riding together.

Be Inspired!

LIFE

I was just sitting and thinking about life and my life. And a word that is resonating with me is, Transition. Now I never take a word at face value especially if it's resonating with me. So, after research, I found that this word has several meanings. There are at least 3 Hebrew words for transition. 1. Ma'avar, which means to "crossover". Which also has a root Me-avar or "from the past". 2. Shinui, which literally means "change". 3. Chiluf that is translated "move on" or "exchange". So, these definitions could realistically have negative and positive meanings. Truth is, we are always in transition. Sometimes we are an active participant, and sometimes by default. Is life right, or wrong, or good, or bad, or fair, or unfair? I don't know. I do know that I have a choice in my actions today. I choose to be an active participant in MY transitions. There is a biblical passage found in 2 Kings 7:3 that says, "The men were in bad shape, but they asked themselves, shall we just sit here until we die?" A simple prayer, "God please grant that all my transitions be wise and constructive bridges!"

Be Inspired!!

POWER

The word Power has several definitions. Let's examine a couple. 1. The ability to do something. 2. Being able to direct or influence the behavior of others or the course of events. 3. Move with great speed or force. It comes from the Latin word " posse" which means "be able". We all have or had areas in our life where we needed these very definitions to be real for us. And then there are those areas that we cannot seem to overcome. Somebody needs to know right now that the same power that freed you from abuse, from lying, stealing, from hanging out in the streets, from addictive behavior, or whatever you were in bondage to, still works. That is the indisputable, irrefutable, incomparable power of God. He's Able!

Be Inspired

FISH TANK

I recently purchased a fish tank. I did this for one, because of ADD, and two, because I am still working on being selfless. Well any who, I had very limited knowledge of taking care of fish or maintaining a fish tank. I'm thinking just get the right food and feed them regularly. Wrong! So, I have 4 fish, all are different types; A Pacu, an Oscar, a Goldfish, and an Algae Eater. By observation, I have found out how they operate. The last two named came with the tank and they are the biggest. When I put the other two in the tank the Oscar right away started palling around, you see one you see the other. The Pacu went off into a corner by himself and he stayed there. The Algae eater attached itself to a rock and appeared to never move. All this happened while the light in the fish tank was on. For a few days, I kept the light on because I was amazed at how everything seemed so normal. Then, I decided to turn the light out. When I did, I discovered that things were not the same when the lights went out, the fish acted differently. The Algae eater moved from place to place in the tank and did his business, the Oscar and the Goldfish separated, and the Pacu was no longer hiding in the corner. How many of us are like these fish? As long as the light is shining on us, we are one way, but change when we think no one is looking. Someone is always looking. God sees you wherever you are and whatever you are doing.

Be Inspired!

MARLON PERKINS

Some of you are old enough to remember National Geographic, a show that used to come on where the main character was Marlon Perkins, whom I thought was one of the smartest men I ever known. The dialogue went something like this, "Hi this is Marlon Perkins." I'll sit safely up here in the shade of this eucalyptus tree as my tour guide Jim wrestles that giant anaconda to extract that most deadly venom. " That is how some of us dangerously live our lives, listening to unwise counsel either from external influences or from our own minds. Psalms 1:1 says, "Don't walk in the counsel of the ungodly."

Be Inspired!

CONVERSATIONS

In the commission of my job, I come in contact with people from all nationalities, races, ages, sexes, economic situations, and belief systems. I've had all different types of conversations from birth to death. Sometimes these people go days, weeks, and months without interacting with other people on a social level. I feel so very honored to be in the position to be sometimes nothing more than an ear. I believe people are placed in our lives all the time to allow us to be selfless, considerate, compassionate, giving, and most of all show love. There is a biblical passage found in 1Corinthians 13:13 that says " Three things will last forever faith, hope, and love and love is the greatest of these three.

Be Inspired!

TRUST

This whole week I had a thought that I wanted to share for inspiration. I want to preface this by saying I never write an inspiration with anyone as my focal point they are always about me. This question came to me, "Does God trust me and how do I know He trust me?" Here is an illustration of this question. When I was younger, I saw people driving cars and said I wanted to do that someday, but I wasn't old enough, or big enough, or smart enough. So as all the reasons, in my mind, left for not being able to drive, I said, "I'm ready." Then I had to go before the chairman of the board, my mother. She had to give her approval. First, she would start me off with small stuff like boy stop asking so much. Then she would say just go outside and start the car. I was also required to go to Drivers Ed and pass with a permit. Do y'all remember that Drivers Ed brake? This was not a quick process, but necessary. Then she finally let me drive, of course, she was in the passenger seat. Finally, she let me loose on my own. I messed up a few times because I was hard-headed, and not paying attention. As time passed, I became responsible and was able to get my own car and follow the rules without supervision, "Point Made." There is a biblical passage found in Matthew 25:23 that says, "You have been faithful over little and now I will give you more." With that being said, does God trust you?

Be Inspired!

FAVOR

I want to approach today's inspiration by first giving some definitions. Over-generous preferential treatment, an act of kindness beyond what is due or usual, give unfairly preferential treatment to and work to the advantage of. A biblical definition of the same word is, gaining approval, acceptance, or special benefits or blessings. All of these definitions are a result of Prayer and Righteous living. Not to be confused with perfection or a state of being without fault. The word of the day is FAVOR. So, as it turns out Favor is fair.

Be Inspired!

GRATEFULNESS

When I left home this morning, I went to work. I got into my work vehicle, right away I began to pray didn't really have a whole lot of words. As I was praying, in my mind I began to look back over my life at some of the situations that I had been delivered from and out of. You talking about a real sense of gratefulness to the point where I shed a tear. Nobody knows like the individual where they were or what they really went through. As I rode down the road another 5 miles I came upon this accident. I thought to myself, "I could have been me." God still has me covered. Be grateful for everything. God is good even better than you know!

Be Inspired!

SPURGEON

One of the greatest preachers of our time, inspired by God, to preach the gospel, was a man by the name of Charles Spurgeon. There are many such men and women, but I mentioned him because of some research I was doing. I found out some interesting facts about him; one was, he was an extremely gifted speaker and expository preacher. In the 1800's he preached to very large audiences as a young man in his teens. The thing about Spurgeon that really caught my attention was even though he naturally had all this going for himself, he understood that the most important thing he could do was pray. He preached with large crowds of people in the sanctuary. He asked all of them to pray and there were at least 150 men in the basement under the pulpit praying also as he proclaimed the gospel. Prayer is indispensable and imperative. One of Spurgeon's quotes about prayer is, "We know not what prayer cannot do", another is "Anything which makes us pray is a blessing."

Be Inspired!

IMAGE

I was having a dialog with a young man just the other day about the ills of the world. That's a current and relevant topic. We both agreed that what is missing in the world, especially among the people that claim to be God's people is IMAGE. Please bear with me. There is a biblical passage found in Genesis 1:26. It starts off by giving a precursor to the ability to do something. It says, "Then God said let us make man in our IMAGE and our Likeness". There it is right there, we have focused more on the Likeness of God and gotten out of the IMAGE of God. The difference is Likeness to God refers to an outward appearance. Another way of saying that is, we go to church, we pay tithes, we serve on various committees, we even dress a certain way. All of that adds up to the Likeness of God. Now the IMAGE of God would be an optical depiction (illustration) of what God would look like in physical form. Since God is spirit then He can't look like a 20 thousand seat cathedral, or a 50-million-dollar life center and so on. I believe the IMAGE of God is LOVE. So, does the condition of the world today look like we are in the IMAGE of God or the Likeness of God? Once we get back not only to the Likeness of God but also the Image of God, we can fix the ills of the world. Ask yourself, am I living in the IMAGE of God or am I just in His LIKENESS?

Be Inspired!

FAT-FREE

I'll have to admit I'm a gadget type guy. I like all the bells and whistles of a thing. I want the latest this and the latest that when it comes to gadgets. That's cool but, the thing about that is you never get to experience the fullness of one thing because you move on to the next thing to fast. As I'm writing this I have to pause and say to myself, "Self is that you talking?" Lol, Hopefully, I'm not by myself. Anyway, the point I'm getting at is about starting and finishing. It is probably better to not start, than to start and not finish. Finishing something or seeing it all the way through has rewards like nothing else. There is a biblical passage that references this found in James 1:4. Says, "Let perseverance finish its work so that you may be mature and complete, not lacking anything."

Be Inspired!

PAIN

I believe besides Love, Pain is the greatest motivator known to man. Pain can come in several forms, whether it be physical or mental. It also can have many sources, i.e. Food, Finances, Fun, Friends, Failures, Faking the Funk, and yes, I'm talking about sources of pain. There are so many things that can cause you pain. The other thing that makes pain significant is the level. Some people like me have very low tolerances to pain, and there are those of us who thrive off the pain. When my daughter is going through painful situations, I have a go-to question that I ask her, and that is " HOW LONG CAN YOU SIT ON THE HEAD OF A NAIL?" The simple answer is until the pain gets to be too great. In my life, I have experienced pain from many sources and I'm here to tell you that the best medicine for the pain that I received was a steady dose of God. When I got that dose, I didn't have to call anyone else, God is the "Ultimate Pain Reliever". Unlike man's medicine, it's not experimental, but supernatural, it's not temporary, it's eternal. It's not only a pain reliever it's multipurpose in its function. Whatever your pain or tolerance for pain, God can fix it.

Be Inspired!

HEALING

Recently I was cooking some turkey wings. I hadn't cooked in a while, but that was by choice. So, I gathered all my ingredients and prepared for it. I got everything just right and put my gourmet dinner in the oven and went on doing whatever else I had going on. All great cooks know, "A watched pot won't boil". At this point you might be saying, "What does that have to do with healing?" Well nothing, LOL, but here it is, once the seasonings started smelling and my nose got full, I went to check on my creation. As I opened the oven and went to pull the dish out, I screamed with a loud cry, oh s---, no I didn't curse I don't think. Needless to say, I burned my hand. I went through several stages with that burn, but after a few days, I stopped worrying about it and then I stopped thinking about it. Until one day, I looked at my hand and realized that it was completely healed. I don't even know when it happened, I just know it did. That's how it is with us Healing is coming, we just don't know when and we don't know how. God's timing is unmatched.

Be Inspired!

STICKS & STONES

Sticks and stones will break your bones, but words will never hurt you. I don't care what you say about me as long as you don't touch me. You made your bed hard now you have to lay in it. A bird in hand is always better than two in the bush. These are some of the old analogies that most of us were taught growing up and made them part of our inner-core belief system.

Well, come to find out they were just passed down untruths. Truth is words are far more dangerous than they are given credit for. They have the power over your very life, not to mention the quality of your life. It would behoove you to be mindful of words. Speaking of that bed, man if the bed is too hard, get out of it, or should I say if the situation is not right and it can't be fixed get out. Finally, the bird; some people have had the bird in their hand so long they have choked the life out of it. It won't fly, can't sing, and don't nobody else even want it. He, who never takes a chance, never has a chance. Carve your own path.

Be Inspired!

TRANSITION

Because we are all always going through one thing or something, I came across this today. The word transition is defined as a period or process of changing from one state or condition to another. It comes from the Latin word "Transpire", which means to Go Across. There is a biblical passage found in Mark 4:35. It says, "On a particular day, Jesus knowing what his disciples had need of, got in a boat with them and said to them, *Let us go to the other side*." When a great storm came and began to test their faith, it was as if they forgot the power they had with them (Jesus). When they got caught up in their human senses, (hearing, seeing, feeling) it was only when they realized they couldn't control their particular situation they reconnected to the power source that was already with them, that their situation began to change and they were able to go to the other side, cross over, or TRANSITION.

Be Inspired!

FAITHFUL

Faith to believe, faithful, adherence, constant, reliable, or steady. So now when the 2 come together, you believe in something so strong that it becomes more than an event. That object of belief becomes a part of you, or you become one with what you believe. At a glance, to the average rational person is just a normal thing. The residue, ramifications, and rewards of the two are far reaching. People call you dependable, reliable and they believe in you. You have stability, you are rooted, and you have direction. More important than all of those admirable things, you please God and is called righteous. There is a biblical passage found in Hebrews 11:6 that says, "Without faith, it is impossible to please God". Now when you please God all kinds of stuff happen to you and for you.

True story, I have been faithful in my belief that these posts were inspired by God so it's something that I do. So, I am walking through the airport and Anthony Hamilton walks up on me. After greeting him I ask him if I can give him a 7-second pitch (that I didn't have), about my vision for a new business that I am starting. God spoke through me in 7-seconds. He gave me his contact information and of course I gave him mine.

Get Ready, Be Ready, Stay Ready.

Be Inspired!

WORD HOMONYMS

Word Homonyms are words that sound alike but have different meanings. Homophones are a type of homonym that also sound alike and have different meanings but have different spellings. HOMOGRAPHS are words that are spelled the same but have different meanings, in essence, words are like people. First of all, they have the same prefix, "Homo" which means "same or akin to", secondly, they perform the same according to the above-mentioned definitions. When you come to realize that words are not like you, but they are you. They are the reason you exist, and they have power over you, life takes on new meaning. It wasn't until the word spoke that you came into existence. Genesis 1:26. Then in John1:1 it tells you that in the beginning was that same Word, which means that when you were created in the image and likeness of God the word was in you. It says even further in Romans 9:10, "If you confess the word you shall be saved, and the Word shall have power over you". The question of the day, what does the Word mean to you?

Be Inspired!

TRANSPARENCY

Transparency, this word means having thoughts, feelings, or motives that are easily perceived. This does not mean that you have to tell people everything. However, it does mean that what you tell them should be real. So, yesterday as I was traveling along a portion of highway doing my normal 10 miles over the speed limit, listening to inspirational music, but extremely tired. I fell asleep, I was so asleep I didn't feel or hear myself leave the highway. When I opened my eyes, I was in the ditch, still doing my usual 10 miles over the speed limit, which was 65, you can imagine the surprise on my face when I opened my eyes. At that moment the car started to go into a spin. I did not once think to brake or take my foot off the gas. The first and only thing that came to my mind was to call on the matchless name of Jesus. I said, "Jesus!" three times. When I said, "Jesus", the third time the car angled back toward the highway, straightened up and I kept driving to my destination. No dents, scratches, bumps, or bruises. The transparent part of this inspirational message is, I'm not ashamed to tell anyone that I don't have it all together, but I called on Jesus and He not only heard, but al understood my cry.

Be Inspired!

CRUTCH

I was having one of those daddy-daughter talks with Britini Feltus, and to get to the point, she mentioned the term "Life Cheerleader". The word crutch instantly came to mind, but not in a bad way. Crutches are an aid used in a process. If you need them, you are in the phase of the process that you are weight bearing but you can't walk on your own without assistance. Now when you get the crutches you have the understanding that they are temporary and used as a means to get you to the next level of your healing. They were never meant to be permanently used. That's a problem for a lot of people. Instead of moving on to the next phase of their treatment they become dependent on something temporary. Oooh weee, been there done that. Push through the pain of the process so you can do what Jesus told the man in the biblical passage John 5:8 "Take up your mat orthotics thing you've been leaning on (crutch) and walk". Today is your day,

Be Inspired!

REVENANT

This is a French word which means "Coming Back". It is defined in English as a person who has returned, especially supposedly from the dead. "Don't call it a comeback" (LL Cool J). We have all experienced or experiencing death in some way or being dead in some way. Whether it be dead in finances, dead in a relationship, emotionally dead, spiritual death, or socially dead. Let's look at the differences in the French definition and the English one. One says coming and the other says one who has already returned. Here's another perspective. Jesus rolled up on a man that was in a grave (dead) and spoke to a dead situation; you know the storyline of John 11:44. He first spoke to the man, "Come Out Of That Dead Situation!" Then He said to the things that had him bound, those dead things, "Loose that man and let him go."

Be Inspired!

PERSEVERE

I usually give the word before the definition, Let's switch it up. "To continue in a course of action even in the face of difficulty or with little or no prospect of success". Some of you might struggle with the right word to use as the definition. But let's take it out and look at it. When the doctor told you there is nothing else, they can do for you. When your support system was nonexistent. When you had absolutely NO money. When you became homeless. When friends told you to give up on that vision, dream, or goal. When you got pregnant and knew you still needed an education. When you went to college with two outfits and $40. When you battled depression but still had to manage your life in public. When you were addicted to drugs and/or alcohol but something way down on the inside would not let you give up. When that relationship didn't work out for the fourth-time. When you felt like no one was there not even God. Through all that you are still standing. It wasn't pretty but you are still here alive and well. That word my friends is **PERSEVERE**. There is a biblical passage found in James 1:3-4. It says, "Hey my brother/sister you do know that when you been through the fire, it builds up your ability to stand and you won't be no chump". **PERSEVERE**.

Be Inspired!

LET GO

I was telling a friend a true story about me, just maybe it will help someone else. When I was in the eighth-grade I thought I was a snazzy dresser. At my eighth-grade graduation, I had on what I thought was the baddest pair of shoes. The shoes were navy/gray. You couldn't tell me anything. Fast forward, when I went to college four years later, I still had the shoes, but at this point, I couldn't even fit the shoes. About six months later, I ran into a situation where I had to get rid of some things. Do you know I struggled with getting rid of those shoes? I couldn't wear them, they had lost their value, and I didn't feel the same about them. I was just holding on to the shoes. Here is the kicker, even when I got rid of the shoes, I found myself comparing new shoes to them. Those shoes are just old memories now

Be Inspired!

A SOLDER'S STORY

This is a must read, don't just glance over this one. When I choose a word or topic to speak on, several things come into play: 1. I want to be relevant. 2. I want to say something. 3. Transparency is important. 4. Last but not least, I want to ensure that God is present. So, this topic a soldier's story came to me because of my own ongoing battles. Soldier's origin is Latin, the word was Solidus. It was used in reference to something solid. Another way to define this is Warrior, which comes from a French word that means to make war. I promise I'm going somewhere. One other term for soldier is Combatant, This word in its English translation means "Someone that is engaged in the war". Most of us fit these definitions of a soldier. So here it is, your story should read, As a soldier, I was solid in every sense of the word. I was a Warrior and when it was time, I made war against the enemy that came against my family, my mind, my finances, my relationships, my time, my body, and most of all my spiritual well-being.

A SOLDIER'S STORY CONT'

Finally, I was a Combatant actively engaged in the war that was made." I told those enemies don't come for me. Psalms 118:11, "Though hostile nations surrounded me, I destroyed them all with the authority of the LORD."

Be Inspired!

DEATH

Death, one of the worst parts of life for some, and for others it's the welcomed end to a long or short period of suffering. I personally have experienced loss on a great scale, especially by recently losing my dad. Because I was in a different place in my life emotionally, it was devastating to me. I think one of the most devastating things about it was that intellectually, I understood that we all have to die someday in some way, I was simply not prepared. I don't believe that you can be prepared emotionally for that type of loss. I am saddened to hear of the passing of family, Facebook friends, and people in general. I am human; I have emotions, so I grieve. This is the same for each reader of this inspirational post. Today it's me, tomorrow it's someone you know, and then it's your turn. There are really no words or deeds, even though they are appreciated, that ease the process. However, there is one thing that helped me. That was a relationship with God. Over time it gave me peace that surpassed my understanding. I'm not saying you have to know God as I do or even worship Him as I do, but I do recommend that you develop your own relationship with the God of your understanding. He "WILL" give you peace!

Be Inspired!

CHRISTMAS

Wow, another major holiday is here. I can remember growing up looking forward to this epic event called Christmas. No other day compared. Birthdays weren't even as big. As I got older the rhetoric began to change. I started hearing things like, "Christmas is just another day." "It's not about me, it's about the kids", and "Jesus is the reason for the season." Now I'm an adult with children and grandchildren. My rhetoric has changed as well. It's not that I don't like the holiday or the gifts that come with it, or even the getting together telling all those lies. I now understand how wasteful it all is. Many will suffer until tax time and some well beyond that, and really why wait until the end of the year to become a cheerful giver. In some circles that's called "Fronting or Stunting". I guess what I'm saying is give whenever possible, give out of your needs and not your abundance, and don't forget my gift this year, LOL. Seriously, if you are a giver you fall under a specific clause from a familiar biblical passage; 2 Corinthians 9:10. When God sees that you are a giver, He will make sure that you won't run out of anything.

Be Inspired!

HAPPY NEW YEAR

My humble prayer is that something, was said or shown to someone, somewhere, that inspired them to think, love, believe, try again, live a better life, forgive, smile, eat better, be proactive, take the high road, be a giver, pray more, be a friend, become selfless, be creative, don't give up, and don't give in. Talked through my own personal circumstances, issues, and concerns, used you all as sounding boards. Received corrective and helpful feedback. Developed and grew as a father, a friend, a man, and Man of God. This year of inspiration made me realize how connected versus separated we all are. Did I mention I talked about love? I have heard for some time that if you know better, you do better. I don't completely agree with that. I believe that if you know better, then because of that information, doing better becomes a choice. In this New Year coming to some, make it your business to Live, Laugh, and Love ❤. But most of all put God first.

Be Inspired!

A GOOD REPUTATION

How do you know me? I met a very famous man several months ago. When I saw him right away I knew who he was. Even if he had not uttered a word; I would have known who he was. The reason for this is because of what he had done in his life, the way he conducted his business, and he also had a signature move he would make. How many of us are famously known for the same characteristics or should I say, characteristics that make us known? What are they? There is a biblical passage found in Proverbs 22:1 that says, "A good reputation is more desirable than great wealth." Here it is Love God, Love Yourself, and Love your neighbor, and that's how I'll know you.

Be Inspired!

GOD GOT YOU

Whether it is family, friends, buddies, associates or whatever titles the people in your life may hold. Don't wait for them to confirm, support, affirm, agree, or see your idea, passion, vision, dreams, or goals. Most people will only support you if it doesn't cost them anything but a prayer. Even Peter, when asked if he knew Jesus said, "NO", for fear of the beat down. If God gave you the Vision, He will certainly give Provision to carry it out.

Be Inspired!

INTERNAL REVIEW

There are times when we are talking about the solution, at the same time being a major part of the problem. This is a matter of internal affairs. This term is used to describe a department that does an investigation on its own members. Now in order to investigate members of your own body or group, you have to be above reproach yourself. We all have issues that need investigation. So, when it comes to an internal review of ourselves, which one of us is by himself qualified? There is however a solution. Psalms 51 addresses this problem in its entirety. It talks about acknowledgment to God that you are the problem. It talks about asking for forgiveness from God and finally it talks about the outcome of the two. God handles internal affairs and fixes the problem (you).

Be Inspired!

GANG AFFILIATION

Today I want to talk about Gangs or gang affiliation. They have been around since forever. There are some very familiar gangs in the world. I don't want to name any because this is less about the gang and more about the members of the gang. Let me digress a little and define what a gang is. A gang is defined as a group of people most often associated with criminals but not exclusive to them. The word gang comes from the Old Norse word Gait, which means a pattern of movement of the limbs during locomotion. This pattern of movement is based on speed, terrain, the need to maneuver and energetic efficiency. So now that you know what it means to be in a gang, how do I know you are in a gang or you are just talking like you are affiliated? Glad you asked. Most gangs that people are actually in have signs. Some signs might be the colors, handshakes, or some other gestures. But God says, "The members of His gang will show these signs according to Galatians 5:22, Love, Peace, Joy, Patience, Kindness, Goodness, and Faithfulness". The question is which gang signs are you showing, which set are you repping?

Be Inspired!

LOOK-ALIKE

Look-Alike. In the midst of a personal struggle, this message came to me this morning. Look-Alike. True story, at my job there is a guy that every time he sees me, he says, "Hey man you look just like Coach Croom". From what I hear, Coach Croom was a really popular football coach in Alabama and Mississippi. I've never even seen a picture of this man, but this man is convinced after seeing me and having seen Mr. Croom that we must be related in some way. In the words of the late Bishop Eddie Long, "Watch this, watch this". How many people come into your presence and are convinced that you look like Jesus or must be related to Him? I remember Pastor Jerome telling me years ago that your character is not based on how you see yourself, but how others see you. There is a book in the Bible that never mentions God, but everywhere in the book, you see God.

Be Inspired!

BUT, WAIT

The inspirational message today comes from a very familiar passage in the Bible found in Isaiah 40:31. It starts off saying, "But those that wait on the Lord". Now you really can stop right there and make a valid point. Let's take it out and look at it. The word "But", means that everything that came before it could be done away with or negated. For instance, if you were a liar, thief, murderer, addicted person, or whatever your condition was/is, "But". Now the word "Wait" means to stay where one is or delay action until a particular time or until something else happens. When I was in Navy boot camp, we had a term or command, it was "Mark time". This meant March on the spot without moving forward. Let's put that together. I don't care what happened last night, last week, or last year we need to stand fast and firm and wait on the Lord.

Be Inspired!

NOMADS

Truth of the matter is this, we are all Nomads. This in the Greek means "In search of a pasture". Now, what does that mean? Glad you asked. It simply means that we are all trying to find that place that is just right for us. Whether you are old, young, rich, poor, healthy, sick, bound, free, no matter what you look like, or even where you came from. It really doesn't matter what your religion is, you still fit in the category of a Nomad. Where we err is, we find room in our minds to have no acceptance for the next person, but we want to be accepted. We have no tolerance for the next person, but we want to be tolerated. We are quick to point out other's shortcomings, but don't want anybody in our business. There is a biblical passage found in Matthew 7: 2-5. It talks about you judging me, but not considering your own judgment and you looking at the speck in my eye, but do not consider the plank in your eye. It says you are a hypocrite. Hey, look we are all Nomads. If we see similarities versus differences, maybe then we can have some hope for unity.

Be Inspired!

THE MIND

I have written these inspirational posts for nearly 4 years. I talked about everything from peace, love, joy, and happiness. I have spoken about family, friendship, and living. There have been inspirations about the economy, the ecosystem, and evolution. I mentioned politics, police brutality, and people in general. I have always tried to tie in some biblical passage or reference to one. Talked about giving and financial stability, health, and dying. Direction, destination, and destiny have been topics. I have tried to remain relevant, reasonable, and reflective. Most of all I've talked about God. But there is another topic I need to discuss because I believe it's probably the most important of all topics. The "Mind" is defined as the element of a person that enables them to be aware of the world and their experiences, to think, and to feel; the faculty of consciousness and thought. The Mind is not your brain. The Mind is thoughts which governs the brain. What this means is without the Mind, all, and I mean all, of the aforementioned stuff, is meaningless to a person. You have heard it said, "The Mind is a terrible thing to waste".

The Mind is the seat of everything you are, think, and do. Nothing happens to you, through you, or by you before it happens in your mind. God uses your Mind to get to you. The devil or the enemy uses that same Mind. The Bible says that this Mind must be renewed, transformed, steadfast, and unmovable, focused, purified, sanctified, holy. It says in Philippians 2:5-11, "The same Mind that Christ had you should have". Today examine yourself (Your Mind).

Be Inspired!

BACKSLIDING

Not very many alive can say that they haven't been through anything. To those who can honestly say they haven't, to them I say keep living. One of my biggest fears, because of the magnitude of my situations that had me bound, is backsliding. This is defined as going back to a situation, place, or thing. I need to make this disclaimer also; there is a difference between abstinence and freedom. So, if you are just taking a break because of being tired, consequences, or confinement, then you are probably still in bondage, just chillin. But freedom means that you have been relieved of compulsion, obsession, and desire. Freedom is something that is not free and needs to be maintained and respected. There is a biblical passage found in Luke 21:36. It says, "Always be watching and paying attention, also stay prayed up, so that you will have a defense against situations and circumstances that will occur."

Be Inspired!

FORMER

Let's look at the word Former. It is defined as, "Having previously filled a particular role or been a particular thing". The reason I chose this word is because I look at the condition or state of man and myself. There is so much going on. You name it and somebody is doing it. Scheming, shaming, lying, drug abusing, gambling, gang banging, over eating, or over shopping, just to name a few. I myself have been party to many negative things and to be honest some things I am still working through, but God. There is a biblical passage found in 1 Corinthians 6:11 that says, "And that is what some of you were doing also, but because you called on God you were changed and justified". This says that whatever condition or situation your present state is, there is a remedy. As the saying goes, "I'm not where I'm going to be, but thanks to God I'm not where I used to be". Seek and you shall find, ask and you shall be told, and knock and the door shall be opened.

Be Inspired!

DREAMS

Dreams are extensions of your waking thoughts, fears, concerns, emotions, and problems. They are a visual picture of what's going on in your mind. I am not sure how my dream will inspire you today, but I felt led to share. I was in a dimly lit room; it was dinner time. I was sitting at a table; the table was round with a few chairs around the table. There were other guests standing around the table but there were not enough chairs for everyone. I could not see the faces of the people because of the lighting, but I could hear their request to be seated. There was a center cut out in the table, that's where I was seated. The food that was prepared was that of the highest quality. The table was set like nothing I have ever seen. In the dream, I was saddened that all who had come to dinner, could not join me in this high-quality meal. I remember getting a phone call and saying, "I don't want to wake up because I want to know who got to sit at the table". My interpretation is, there is a place that only a select few can join you, so choose carefully.

Be Inspired!

SALVATION & MATURITY

Every now and then a dose of reality is needed to get the point across to people. The truth of the matter is people don't always want to hear the truth or reality.

Most time people don't want to change or stop what they are doing, they just don't want the consequences of what they are doing. Speaking for Felt, if I had not gotten caught, felt bad, or hurt folk in the process, I would still have been doing some of that foolishness I was doing. That's where two things come into play and in this order; Salvation and Maturity. Salvation is defined as deliverance from ruin or loss and deliverance from sin and its consequences brought about by faith in God. Maturity is defined as sensible, levelheaded, responsible, wise, and developed in thought and action. God changes the heart and the mind so that you think and act different and in turn get different consequences. 2 Corinthians 5:17 says, "Once you have gotten rid of the zero and gotten with the hero (God), all that old foolishness is gone, and new stuff begins".

Be Inspired

RESCUED

On my job, I come in contact with people from all walks of life. There's a woman I met who has ten dogs. Most of them are rescues, and some just came because the others were there. They were in varying conditions when she got them. Some were very unhealthy and even near death, but all were taken care of and nursed to health by her. She says that it is a labor of love. Truth be told this is a real-life analogy that reminds me of myself and lots of folks I know. God rescued us from varying conditions and nursed us back to healthy productive members of society. Because of the light that now shines through us others will come to know God. Be a shining light this year someone else needs rescuing.

Be Inspired

HISTORY & WISDOM

I had the honor of meeting an 84-year-old Korean War veteran a couple of days ago. It was great for me because I love history and wisdom. So right away, I started asking questions. The first question I asked was his age. From then on, he took over the conversation. It was unsaid but understood that he needed to talk, and I needed to listen. I bet y'all want to know what he said, and here it is, he told me some old things. He had an incredible memory. He talked about the war in detail and he reaffirmed some things. He hit me with the "When I was a little boy the old folk would say..." So that hasn't changed. Then he said that he had been a lot of places and seen a lot of things, he learned a lot of things, made some mistakes and got some things right. He has very few possessions left, but he is at peace. In conclusion, he said the best piece of advice he could give me, "To live every day until I died and don't forget God". That message is for everyone.

Be Inspired!

WASTING TIME

I was recently in the store doing what has become one of my past times, now I know you think I'm about to say shopping, well that's not it. Over the last few years, I've become a certified people watcher. Now I'm not watching in a perverted way. I just find myself paying attention to detailed information. Don't act like y'all aren't doing it also, because I've seen people watching me watching them. It's crazy how we can actually spend valuable waking moments of our day engaged in activities that at the end of the day won't benefit us one bit. Now I used myself and something I do or did as an example of wasting time. Take a moment and examine your own lives, be honest with yourselves, ask the important questions. Where and why am I wasting time when it is so little left? It's not like you can do like the Senators and reclaim the time. There is a biblical passage found in John 9:4 that says, "Man, you don't have but so much time to get something done, put in some work while you can".

Be Inspired!

OBSTACLES

Obstacles, Adversity, Money, Sickness, People, The Enemy (internal/external), Temptation, and YOU are just a few examples of obstacles that will keep you from getting something done, reaching a goal, or reaching your full potential in life. However, if you place and keep your thoughts on these three things your reward will be great; Faith, Hope, and Love. Faith is the substance of things hoped for and the evidence of things not seen. Faith comes in two parts, belief and actions. Faith says when those things (obstacles) that I mentioned earlier show up, you push pass them. Faith will move God to act on your behalf. Hope, it is defined as a feeling of expectation and a desire for something to happen. Hope is not used for what you can see, but rather on the unseen. Why hope for a dollar when it's in front of you. Lastly Love. So many things have been used to describe love. Love is kind, patient, long-suffering, it doesn't envy, it doesn't boast, it's not proud, doesn't keep a record of wrong, doesn't think evil, never gives up and it has the other two wrapped up in it. These three things overcome obstacles.

Be Inspired!

PAIN vs. TRUST

As a person that inspires on a regular, I usually see inspirational messages everywhere. So, I'm in a therapy session chopping it up with the therapist and I ask him if I can walk and he looks at me and says, "Yes you can". He then said, "What's stopping you from walking is you don't trust the procedure you just had". So, in my mind I say, "I'm going to prove him wrong". I stand straight up and raise my foot to take a step and the first hint of pain I say, "Oooh!", and immediately back to the walker I go. Now I know I talk about pain, but this is about trust versus pain. He that has an ear let him hear.

Be Inspired!

PUBLIC SUCCESS/PRIVATE FAILURE

"Public Success/ Private Failure". Makeup on, hair done, dressed just right. Being in the limelight and getting public praise, who doesn't like the attention. Everyone hitting the like button saying amen looks good for your public image. We post pictures of our new cars, our newborn babies, talk about the new job, the raise, and the vacation we just went on. We want everyone to see the appearance of health, wealth, and prosperity. There is another you that no one knows about. Depression, low / no self-esteem, thoughts of suicide, abusive relationship, inappropriate relationship, no support system, addiction, history of family mental illness, molestation, struggles with faith, and trust issues. You wake up the next day and go back into acting mode, hoping nobody can figure it out before your deliverance comes. There is a biblical passage 1 Corinthians 6:11(New Living Translation), "Some of you were once like that. But you were cleansed; you were made holy; you were made right with God by calling on the name of the Lord Jesus Christ and by the Spirit of our God. He hears your moaning and groaning for relief".

Be Inspired

LIVING

One day, I heard a good friend of mine say they wanted to live before they die. They were up in age which, means that they have been around for some time. I said to myself, "Self you mean to tell me there could possibly be a whole lot of people on the earth that are doing nothing more than existing, going through the motions, and faking the funk?" Most people that you encounter have the appearance of life. They dress nice, they speak well, they have nice things, they are in the stores spending money, go to work, put their children through college, they are doing all the things that look like living. Then I said to myself, "Self maybe living is more than just performing a series of ritualistic acts. Maybe living is about coming to know God and establishing a relationship".

Be Inspired!

TEMPTATIONS

Temptation is a desire to do something or have something that is wrong or unwise. Another word that can be used for temptation is Lure. This is defined as something that is used to tempt a person, seduce, or lead astray from one's true course. Most people relate lures to fishing. Well, any good fisherman knows that without the right lure, you will be fishing in vain; some fish will only bite on certain bait. The fisherman has to know what a particular fish likes. He learns that through trial and error. How does that pertain to us? Thanks for asking. We can't be tempted or lured by something that we aren't already attracted to. Temptation has two sources, external and internal. Without prayer, power, and protection against lures and temptations, we sometimes find ourselves on the losing side. Thank God for His Forgiveness, Grace, and Mercy that are new and fresh every day.

Be Inspired!

WORDS

I must confess that I have a love for words. There is something about them (words) that really fascinate me. They define, they describe, they build, they have the ability to move people, they have the power to change the mind, and they can change circumstances. They are used consciously and subconsciously by everyone; they are sometimes spoken and sometimes written. As it turns out, they are the building blocks of our very existence. There is a word that I just became aware of that really resonates with me. Please excuse the size of the word. "Geosynchronous" is the word. It's a scientific word that deals with satellites. It references a satellite or orbit of a satellite. This in everyday terms means that there is a satellite that is programmed to focus on a particular or specific area on earth. It moves at the same speed as the earth, monitors every detail of that particular area, and records all the data pertaining to that specific area. All this happens in a 24-hour period. You might be asking yourself, "What does this word have to do with inspiration on today?" Well, it should inspire you to think of the "Geosynchronous orbit" that God makes around us on a daily basis, bring awareness to the "Everywhereness" of God! There is a biblical passage found in Hebrew 4:13 it says, "There is nothing and no one hidden from the sight of God, whom we must all give an account".

Be Inspired!

CHILD-LIKE

There is a biblical passage found in 1 Corinthians 13:11 that says, "When I was a child my speech was that of a child, my thoughts were infant-like and my understanding was child-like also, but when I became a man, I put away childish things". At a glance, this can be interpreted as something that just takes place over time or with age. A deeper look shows that this man was an active participant in the change in his life. He understood that his old way of thinking was no longer beneficial, his speech or the way he spoke had to change to be current with the new man he had become. When his thoughts, conversation, and understanding changed he was able to put away those childish things. "Become" is a word that simply means "begin to be".

Be Inspired!

MY NEPHEW JUELZ

FAILING AND FALLING

Failing and Falling, two words with similar meanings, but they are different. Fail is defined as "Being unsuccessful in achieving one's goal, neglecting to do something, or even breaking down, ceasing to work". Fall is defined as "Moving downward without control, a sudden uncomfortable decent, or decrease, decline, diminish, dwindle". The difference I see in the two is that failing has a connotation of conviction, which deals with the state of mind or belief system. Falling has more connotation of condemnation, which deals more with gloom, doom, right, wrong and judgment. There is a biblical passage found in Romans 8:1 that says, "Once you establish yourself with God there is no more condemnation for you". That leaves you left with your beliefs or convictions. I don't know about you, but I would rather be established than doomed!

Be Inspired!

RETROSPECT, INTROSPECT & PROSPECT

This week ended like most weeks, filled with a lot of life, on life's terms, and issues. Three words should permeate our thoughts, the first is the word "RETROSPECT", this is a survey of past time or events, specifically our own. We need to be aware of where we have been, what we have done, and most importantly why we have acted the way we have. The second word is "INTROSPECT", this is defined as looking or examining your own thoughts or feelings at this present time. Present personal inventory, not to be confused with meditative or meditation, which is deep thought about one thing, but not necessarily something personal. The final word is "PROSPECT", the possibility or likelihood of some future event occurring. This word deals with hope, anticipation, probability, and promise. Now to be current, when you know better you have the opportunity to do better and get better.

Be Inspired!

EXPRESSIONS

How many times have you heard the expressions "That was a real eye-opener" or "I bet you didn't see that coming" or even "The hand is quicker than the eye"? All these expressions deal obviously with seeing something new for the first time. I want to suggest that there are at least two very important eye-opening events in the life of every person. The first is the day that you are born. When you open your eyes for the first time, you were in complete darkness, alive but blind to everything around you. As time went on you began to see more and more clearly. Until the day you were brought to the next eye-opening experience. That is the day your eyes were opened to the fact that you were still blind and didn't have the ability on your own to see things the way they really are. This is the beginning of your eye-opening experience with God. (That takes a lot for granted on my part.) So, if your eyes haven't been opened for the second time, stop right now and ask God to open your eyes. There is a biblical passage found in John 9:25 that says, "Whether he be a sinner or not I don't know, but one thing I know, whereas I was blind, now I see".

Be Inspired!

GIVE

Anyone of us would quickly and gladly give something or do some noncommittal act of kindness toward someone we know or even a stranger. The problem with that is, it leaves us the way most of us are, not connected or tied to anyone or anything. It is only when we give not out of our abundance, but out of our need that we begin to be fruitful. What is meant by giving out of our need? Glad you asked! Whatever you have need of in your own life, begin to give that away. If you need Love, give love. If you need happiness, give it. If you need peace, be peaceful, and so on. There is a biblical passage found in Luke 6:38 that says, "Give and it shall be given to you, good measure, pressed down and shaken together and running over, they shall give into your bosom, for with that measure with which ye give it shall be given unto you again."

Be Inspired to give for the right reason!

MYOPIC

The ability to see is tri-fold in nature. It is based on mind, body, and spirit. There is a term or condition that deals with seeing called MYOPIC. It means being short-sighted or near-sighted in every sense, either you need glasses or a new attitude. With this condition, you can't see the whole picture or the big picture. As the saying goes "You can't see the forest for the trees". You have an attitude of indifference and/or intolerance. All this is a direct result of a process called erosion, usually related to the earth surface. Erosion can be defined as gradual destruction of something by internal and or external forces over time. There is a biblical passage found in Songs of Solomon 2:15 that says, "It's the small foxes that destroy the vines." In other words, it's the little things that wear away at our ability to see in a tri-fold way. My prayer is Lord open my eyes that I may see clearly and not Myopically.

Be Inspired

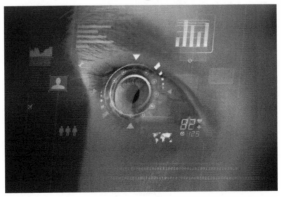

THE 3 D's

There are three main D's in life. Each one is different for us all. First is DIRECTION. Direction is defined as "The course, along which someone or something moves, and the management and guidance of someone or something." As it pertains to us, we are not on autopilot. I have read somewhere that our steps are ordered and numbered. Direction leads us to a DESTINATION. Destination can be defined as "The place to which someone is going or being sent. There is a place which ends travel, a place of peace and rest. Sometimes it's as simple as just traveling in a direction that just leads you to the house at the end of the day. Your destination will be determined by your direction. The final D is DESTINY. This can be defined as, "The end of everything". The thing about destiny is that we have a more active role in the end result. God, please give me what I need to travel in a DIRECTION that leads me to a DESTINATION that will propel me into the DESTINY that is for me.

Be Inspired!

BATTLES

There are all types of battles that each of us will fight in our lives. We are born fighting to adapt to a new environment. We strive in schools from start to finish, and there are battles with and between friends, loved ones, and financial struggles. But I propose that the greatest battle that any of us will ever be in is the battle of and for our minds. It's the most powerful underused, undermanaged, undervalued tool that we have. There is a biblical passage found in Romans 12:1, 2 that makes reference to the fact that our minds, as a condition of success, have to be transformed. I am the first to say I need more transformation for the battles that I face.

Be Inspired!

COMMUNITY

This time of year makes me think of growing up in Illinois where the winters were brutal and that's a nice way of putting it. I can remember temperatures so far below zero that folks in the south could not even imagine it. Snow up to the wazoo, walking to school in those conditions, and oh yeah, pipes bursting, that was a crazy situation in itself. The thing about all of that's as crazy as it was, we found a way as a community to make it through, over, and around all of the obstacles of the times. I'm convinced now more than ever that it was with the help and guidance of Almighty God. Geographics, people, and times may change in our lives, but we need to keep depending on God to see us through. There is a biblical passage found in Proverbs 3:5-6 that says, "Whatever is going on in your life, don't try to figure it out on your own, consult God and He will guide you through it."

Be Inspired!

TODAY

This day is the most important day of our lives. It has so many implications. For some, it's the end of a night that was filled with more than enough hell. Then there are those that will say that their life-long struggle ended last night. Some folk will proclaim freedom today! It will be devastating for someone today. But the most important thing about today if you are reading this is; it is another opportunity. Make today count. Use this opportunity like it is your last, it just might be!

Be Inspired!

PERSPECTIVE

On my job, I come in contact with people from all walks of life. There is a woman I met who has 10 dogs. Most of them are rescues, but some came just because the others were there. They were in varying conditions when she got them. Some were very unhealthy and even near death, but all were taken care of and nursed to health by her. She says it is a labor of love. Truth be told this is a real-life analogy that reminds me of myself and lots of people I know. God rescued us from varying conditions and nursed us back to healthy, productive members of society. And because of the light that now shines through us, others will come to know God. Be a shining light this year someone else needs rescuing.

Be Inspired!

FORCE

No one is exempt from opposition. From the time we were born, we faced opposition or Force. Getting free from the womb, taking the first breath outside of the womb, learning to walk and talk, all opposing forces. And so, the forces began. Star Wars coined the phrase, "Let the Force be with us", and boy has Force been present. Force is defined as a push or pull upon something resulting from an interaction with something. Whenever there is an interaction between two things there is a Force upon each of them. When the interaction ceases the two things no longer experience the Force. This has been a year in which most of us have met many opposing Forces. But if you have had God on your side you have had what is called a "Force Field". Let's end this year thanking God for protection against opposing Forces. Love conquers all!

Be Inspired!

MIRRORS

Mirrors, they are everywhere, in the bathroom, in the bedroom, in the hallways of your home. They are in stores, in buildings, airports, literally everywhere. When I was a truck driver there were really large mirrors on the truck that were used to see various angles but, there is no rear-view mirror. Anyone who has ever driven a big truck will tell you, with all that you can see, there are still what you call "Blind Spots. Our lives are similar in that way; even though we can see a lot, there are so many things we cannot see, we definitely can't see behind us. Some of us, however, spend valuable time looking in the rear-view mirror of life and the blind spots of life and miss what is in front of us, causing accidents and other damage around us. There is a biblical passage found in Philippians 3:13 that says," It's not that he had arrived, but the main thing was that he wasn't looking at his past, but rather he was looking towards his future." Focus on what is in front of you today.

Be Inspired!

INJURIES

There are some injuries and ailments (physical and mental) that only reveal themselves through the pain that is present because of them. The pain then is not the problem but only a symptom. So sometimes the pain is necessary. The problem still has to be treated. Unfortunately, sometimes to get to the root of the problem, surgery (or some type of procedure) is necessary, which can lead to more pain, which is also necessary. If that resembles anyone's current or future situation, I dare you to tell yourself that after this there will be HEALING, VICTORY, PEACE, FREEDOM, JOY, and LOVE!

Be Inspired

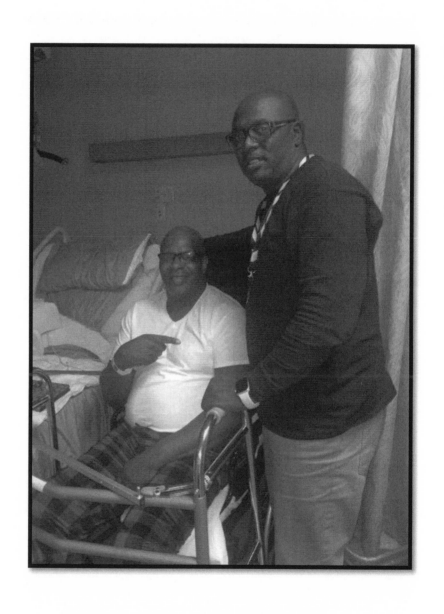

ONE OF MY CLOSE FRIENDS KEVIN

VOICES

We are from the time we are born, surrounded by voices. Voices of our families, friends, teachers, radios, televisions, preachers, and so many other avenues. Please don't be deceived, we are influenced by our environment. Often times, we in some way, if we are not paying attention, will mimic our environment. There is a biblical passage found in Psalms chapter 1, that makes reference to not walking in the counsel of the wicked, and don't be hanging out with sinners, or negative people. Your very existence can depend on the voices that you listen to. Because I have a choice, I pray for strength to allow God's voice to be the loudest in my head and the courage to faithfully follow His lead.

Be Inspired!

TIME

One of the most important undervalued assets we have as humans is Time. We put things off that should be handled in a timely manner. We are chronically late as a people for events, large and small, business or pleasure. You've heard the old sayings, "Why put off for tomorrow what you can do today", or "A stitch in time saves nine", and "Don't be on CP time" LOL. Today is a great time to evaluate for yourself whether you are using or misusing one of the most valuable assets you have been given; TIME. 2Corinthians 6:2 says, "At the right time God heard you crying out to Him and He helped you. That was the day of salvation". That day is now. What perfect timing!

Be Inspired!

PAST

On this and every day we should all have plenty of things to be thankful for. I'm thankful for my past. For if it had not been for the things that I went through; the good, the bad, and the ugly I would not be the man that I am. Am I perfect? No, but I am not on auto pilot either. Also, very thankful for the friends, family, and foes in my life, for they are the instruments by which I am sharpened on a daily basis. Thankful for my present situation or condition because it's the fire that removes the impurities. And most of all I'm thankful for having a relationship with the God of my understanding. For with Him there is an expected end.

Be Inspired!

FLOWERS

There are some flowers, when you get them, come in flower pots that are not meant to house them for their entire existence. If they stay in the pot too long or past their intended time, they can experience complications that can be damaging and sometimes irreparable. We as people sometimes find ourselves or put ourselves in places or situations that we shouldn't be in permanently. We suffer because of our inability or unwillingness to move forward. We become weak, unproductive, and ineffective. We need to be strengthened and mentally renewed in our minds. Philippians 4:13 says, "I can do all things through Christ who strengthens me!" My affirmation is "I'm COMING OUT"

Be Inspired!

WAR

War is defined as a conflict carried on by force of arms, a state or period of armed hostility, or active contention. Unfortunately, we all are at war always in some form or another. Sometimes behind the most peaceful smile there is a waging war. The definition of a Warrior is a person who shows or has shown great vigor, courage, or aggressiveness in an activity, cause, or conflict. There are however, some Wars even the most skill Warriors find themselves less than victorious. There is a biblical passage in Ephesians 6:10-18 that gives some instructions on how to be successful in war. At the end of the passage in verse 18 it says, "Do all this in prayer asking for God's help". Aren't you glad you don't have to do this alone?

Be Inspired!

EYE HAVE NOT SEEN

"The best times of our lives", is a term that resonates different for each of us. At one point I would have said for me it was those high school days (Eastridge), then my college days (Illinois State University). After that the Military (US Navy), you get the point. Many different, but great experiences. There comes a point when all that you have done, seen, heard, and been through still has not filled you or made you whole. For me, when I met God for myself and established my own relationship with Him, I realized life from a different view. There was so much more. It's like being blind and not knowing it until you really begin to see. Thank God today for opening your eyes or ask Him to open your eyes. 1 Corinthians 2:9 says, "What no eye has seen, nor ear has heard, nor the heart of man imagined, what God has prepared for those who love him."

Be Inspired!

INSTABILITY

Instability was a word that rang out in my mind this morning. Let's take it out and look at it. One definition says, tendency to unpredictable behavior or erratic changes of mood. That's a characteristic that can be linked to nature, we all know about the various weather conditions. It can be linked also to animals; they sometimes just flip the script. It can and is most time attributed to us humans. Up one day, down the next, and from one-to-ten in no time at all. We have instability in most areas of our lives at some point or another. The key word in the definition was Tendency. There is however a way of escape from these tendencies. 2 Corinthians 5:17 says, "Therefore, if anyone is in Christ, the new creation has come, the old has gone, the new is here." If you are New, Act New!

Be Inspired!

FREEDOM

There is the biblical account of a woman that was brought before Jesus, to be stoned because of some indiscretions, some areas of her life that she was yet working through. Folks are quick to point out your faults, but because of our inability to out-sin the grace of God, Jesus said then and today, "Those among you without sin and his own issues cast the first stone." He then said something that gave the woman freedom. Not freedom to continue in the same manner but freedom from the bondage of her past. He said to her, "I don't condemn you." When God sets you free you are free!

Be Inspired!

LAWS

There are many laws that govern us as a people. State Laws, Federal laws, Environmental Laws, Social laws, and there are God's laws. One in particular is the law of Reciprocity. This is the practice of exchanging things with others for mutual benefit. Psychologically it means responding to a positive action with a positive action. Spiritually it means what you sow you also reap. To me it means what you want from someone become just that. Whether it be Love, a friend, or support. Be what you need, give and receive it in return.

Be Inspired!

FAVOR

Favor, Fame, and Fortune are very desirable statuses to have in life. Some would even kill to have one or all of these. There is another way to get these things and they will not be temporary. That way is called Faithfulness. One writer said, "without Faith it is impossible to please God". If you please God even your enemies will be at peace with you. He will withhold no good things from you. The cattle on a thousand hills belong to God and He doesn't eat beef so that must be a reward for Faithfulness. Putting your trust in God is the way to success! Live by Faith!

Be Inspired!

BELIEF SYSTEM

You can be from anywhere in life, meaning economically, socially, religiously or not religious at all. You will have a belief system. That belief system was developed as a direct result of your environment. When you think about where you are. If it's not a place that's suitable to you or for you to evaluate to your environment or influences which directly affect your belief system. You will only do what you believe you can, you will only go where you believe you can, and you will only have what you believe you can. Proverbs 23:7 says, "So a man/woman thinks in their heart so are they". God is a proven source of a great influence. Trust Him and live.

Be Inspired!

CONSUMED

Being consumed by a situation, thing, or person can almost take your very life or feel like it sometimes. If you are not in one of these categories right now just think back if it's not too painful and remember when. On the other hand, if you consume yourself with God, He will not take the life out of you but give you life everlasting. Then you won't be looking back but you will be looking ahead. John 10:10 says "That the thief comes to steal, kill, and destroy but I came that you might have life more abundantly". Choose today whether you want to live or die.

Be Inspired!

DIRECTIONS

Directions are for people that are lost. Society has developed a tool to give us direction, it's called a GPS. It speaks to you in a language that you can understand. It guides you to a destination of your choosing, and if you take a wrong turn it can usually get you back on track by rerouting you. Man has tried to copy the technology of God. The difference is God can direct all your paths, He is not limited in where He can guide you. God's power is not limited to electronic or solar energy. He will also guide you into righteousness and truth.

TRAVEL WITH THE RIGHT GPS!

Be Inspired!

PAIN

Pain can be defined as a physical, emotional, or mental response to an equal or opposite action. It is something that every living thing or being including God can experience. It is probably the greatest motivator known to God or man. I asked my daughter one time, "How long can you sit on the head of a nail?" Well the obvious answer to the question is until the pain becomes too much to bear. At some point, inaction will not be an option. Once you have overcome your pain you can become a source of healing for someone else. Somebody needs to know that it is possible to be healed, to be whole, to be free Mind, Body, and Spirit. Who better to tell the story than an overcomer? There is a biblical passage found in Revelations 12:11 that says, "They overcame by the words of their testimony". By sharing your story, you help others as well as yourself.

Be Inspired!

RELATIONSHIP

Today's inspiration is about Relationship. The word relationship is defined as the way two or more concepts, objects, or people are connected or the state of being connected. So, by definition, you can't be in a relationship with anything without being connected to it. You can't be connected to anything without being in a relationship with it. There is a very familiar biblical passage found in Luke 15:11-32 about a young man referred to as the prodigal (a person who is reckless and wasteful with resources) son. He did not respect and appreciate the connection and relationship he had with his father. So, he left the relationship and became disconnected and fell into a bad state, called prodigal. He came to himself and said, "Hold up, wait a minute something isn't right. I got to clean up what I messed up". Imagine being in a relationship with something vital to your existence like oxygen, eating healthy, or just living right, and saying to yourself, "I think I'll go live like a fool". Same concept as a prodigal. God is standing, waiting, knocking, looking, all for you. Ready to restore the Relationship.

Be Inspired!

MY SISTERS, MY DAUGHTER, MY NEICE,
and Two of my GRANDDAUGHTERS

PRAYER

I was just thinking about prayer and how most of mine have been used to get God to change either the things in my life or the people in my life. You know the ones like "God if they aren't going to be good for me remove them" or "God please get me out of this or fix them Lord". Here's a thought, "Lord fix My heart, do an overhaul on My mind, fix My picker, Help Me to see with your eyes". Truth be told, most of the time on some level I am the Problem!

Be Inspired!

ATTACKS

There is an attack or battle going on in your life, whether it be internal, which means that there is conflict going on inside your own mind about everything that concerns you. Or it can even be external, which means there are enemies seen and unseen attacking you on a regular basis. War is real! It behooves each of us to arm ourselves with the proper weaponry to fight the battles. I have personally tried all types of things to triumph in these battles and was defeated. It was not until I found God that I began to realize some victory in my life. So today, if you are someone that keeps coming up on the losing end, be honest with yourself. I recommend that you try God who has an undefeated record in defending His Partners. After all, if you are already losing what do you have to lose by trying something new. If Nothing changes Nothing changes!

Be Inspired!

OLD THINGS PASSED AWAY

There is definitely evidence that people are for the most part creatures of habit. We eat basically the same foods, shop at the same stores, hang around the same people, and pretty much think the same recurring thoughts. The only problem with that is, "If Nothing Changes Nothing Changes". I call that the "Same Ole Syndrome". However, is a possible scenario in which positive change is possible. Develop a concrete relationship with God and He will make your life brand new. 2 Corinthian 5:17 says, "Therefore, if anyone be in Christ. He is a new creation, the old is gone, and the new is present".

Be Inspired!

VISION

Vision, this word is in itself powerful and can be used in many forms. Let's look at a couple of these. First there is "Vision", this simply means being able to see. Then there is "Division", which means to be separated. Also, there is "Envision", which means to imagine as a future possibility. Another is "Revision", which means to revise or rewrite. Now you might ask, "How does these apply to me?" Well, thanks for asking. Without Vision you can't see physically, mentally, or spiritually, which means that you have been Divided or separated from what you could have Envisioned or believed possible for your future. If that is the case, then there needs to be a Revision or rewriting of the prescription to help your Vision. My prayer is God help me to see! Proverbs 29:18 says, "Without Vision the people perish".

Be Inspired!

SEASONS

When it comes to seasons, they are not predicated on your readiness. Winter comes whether you have a coat, boots, and gloves or not. If there is an opportunity that presents itself in your life it comes whether you are ready for it or not. Psalms 1 says, "If you don't walk in the council of the ungodly, nor stand in the path of sinners, or sit in the seat with scornful. In your season you shall produce, and prosper, and be sustained." So, the thing is not if the blessings come it's whether or not you are ready for them. Stop blaming and get your weight up!

Be Inspired!

CHOOSE WISELY

It's true that we need food for survival. We have to be mindful and careful of what we eat. Have you ever been hungry and had a taste for cereal, you set your mind on it and prepare to eat it, only to be feeling some type of way when you find out that the cereal is stale, or the milk is sour? Then you can eat some stuff that will poison your system, they call that food poisoning. You have to be treated for that. It is like that with eating mentally and spiritually also. You can eat or be fed some things that will mess up your mind or make you spiritually sick and find yourself needing to be treated. Choose wisely today what you eat. Matthew 4:4 says, "That man shall not live by bread alone but every word that comes from God".

Be Inspired!

TAKERS, RECEIVERS & GIVERS

If I may, I want to illuminate three things for consideration. Takers, Receivers, and Givers. A taker is a person that gets something by physical or mental manipulation. This person usually wears him or herself out, they run out of provision, people to take from, and they end up in a state of lack and want. Then there is the receiver. This person is also dependent on others, but he or she waits on the gifts of others. Unfortunately, sometimes receiving can lead to a state of lack and want also because it always requires someone to be in place to give. Then there is the giver. This person is one that has more than a taker or a receiver, because in order to give you have to have sustained provision, an endless supply. If you are always giving it can never be said that you don't have. When I became a giver, I began to realize the verse that says, "The Lord is my shepherd and I shall not be in want". You define yourself and what you have by your actions. That my friend is not judging; that's just me thinking!

Be Inspired!

TRY

The definition of the word Try is "to attempt to do or accomplish something." Well, the thing about trying is usually you don't get the satisfaction of completion. You hear people saying all the time "I'm trying, or I'll try to get back with you, I'll give it a college try". Trying gives you a way out by saying at least I tried. It's been my experience that anything that I really ever wanted to do, I did. For Christians and believers of the word Philippians 4:13 says, "I can (Try) all things through Christ who strengthens me". No, it says, "I can DO all things through Christ who strengthens me".

Be Inspired!

CONSIDERATION

"If I can say one thing, to inspire one person, to consider one thing that might need considering, then I will have been purposeful in my consideration of one thing"

"A Felt Original"
Anthony B. Feltus

SURFING

I was able to spend physical time with my son for my birthday. He told me about the "Come Up" that he has been waiting on. I began to tell him about surfing. Of course, I'm not a surfer, but I have seen the movie "Point Break", LOL. In my mind, I related surfing to life, or the "Come Up". I told him that surfers ride waves, but they can't create the waves that they ride. They (surfers) will go to great lengths to find the wave. They will travel great distances to experience the wave. Even before all of this they understand some essentials. First you have to be prepared. That means having the right equipment. You don't go to the water with a tennis racket talking about surfing. Then you have to be clothed with the right gear. There is a biblical passage found in Ephesians 6:11, it says, "Clothe yourself with the whole armor of God". Then there is the waiting part. They have to wait on the wave to come after they have prepared. There is a biblical passage found in Isaiah 40:31, it says, "They that wait upon the Lord shall be rewarded". But you have to wait with the right frame of mind, with expectations, with a watchful eye, and pray.

Be Inspired!

LIVE ABUNDANTLY

Good morning, here's something to kick off the week with. Unfortunately for some and fortunately for others it's time to get on with the business of living. Well Jesus said, "I came that you might have life and it more abundantly." We as people find every opportunity, occasion, and reason to do something to shorten our life and take away from that abundance. One of those ways we do that is by focusing on things that take away from us instead of adding to us. One of those things we focus on is sin. Truth is the wages for sin have been paid. What that means for you is stop trying to pay and make someone else pay for something that has already been paid for and get on with the business of living. Philippians 4:8 says, "Finally my brothers and sisters, whatever is true, whatever is noble, whatever is right, whatever is lovely, whatever is admirable- if anything is praiseworthy - think about such things."

Be Inspired and Live!

UNBELIEF

The power of God has no limitations. You can actually do all things through Christ who strengthens you. There is one thing that will short circuit your success every time. That is UNBELIEF. Matthew 17: 20 says, "He told them it was because of your little faith. I tell you the truth, if you have the faith the size of a mustard seed, you can say to this mountain (your mountain), Move from here, and it will move, and nothing will be impossible for you"!

Be Inspired!

SIGHT vs. FAITH

You might very well be in a place and time in your life where division exist. Another way to say that is double vision. Another way to say that is not having singleness of focus. The truth is sight is important, even more important than sight is faith. John 20:29 says "Blessed(happy) are they that have not seen but still believe". So, begin to speak into your own situation. You have been given that authority. Not name it and claim it but say it and believe it not wavering.

Be Inspired!

HAPPY BIRTHDAY TO ME!

Good morning family and friends. First and foremost, I give God thanks for this day and all it brings. This is the most important day of my life at this point. Last night was like Christmas Eve and today is like Christmas. (You all remember those days?) I went to bed with this thought on my mind. Life will bring you to many first and seconds.... But, only one last thing. There have been 54 Happy Birthday, but one day the timeline for me will read, "RIP, RIH, Farewell, See you when I get there". That's why this day is so important. I have been blessed to be way down and come way up in life, I've lost everything and regained many times what I lost. I've traveled all over the world, recovered from life threatening situations, overcome insurmountable obstacles, and have this testimony about it all. "If it had not been for the Lord who was on my side, who was my crutch to lean on, who carried me when I could not walk, who strengthened me when I was weak, who gave me His unconditional Love, who turned me around when I was going the wrong way, who opened my eyes when I could not see. All praise and thanks to God for the miracle of life".

P.S. Pisces do it better

Be Inspired!

SUPPORT

What is the definition of the word support? Well it comes from two Latin words, sub which translates from below and port which means carry. The English definition of support is to bare all or part of the weight, endure and tolerate, give assistance, encourage, comfort, advocate, and approve. There are so many people, including me, going through so many things right now. From medical issues, financial problems, death of love ones, relationship issues, problems on the job, even issues of a spiritual nature, and so many more. One thing that people are always going to need is support. When you are down, someone to lift you up and not beat you down. Sometimes you might need to be carried and not dropped, other times you will need encouragement, someone to speak for you, to you, or into you. Prayers are always needed. All of these are means of support. Another thing about supporting someone in their time of need is in so doing, you are setting yourself up for your time of need. It's like putting money in the bank. You put it in because you know you are going to need it on a rainy day. Make your investment today for what you will need tomorrow. Today it's me, tomorrow it's your turn. Support someone that's in need.

Be Inspired!

UBUNTU

I had a conversation with my son on yesterday, which has become one of my favorite things as a father. As we were talking, I was reminded of a South African word that a dear friend gave to me. It was like a word of words. When I read the definition I knew it was a gem. Before I tell you what the word is, I want to express how very grateful for you, the reader, of this inspirational message I am. I've encountered many people all over the world that have impacted my life and for that I'm also grateful. I have experienced ups and downs, abundance, lack, sickness, calamity, loss, distraction, disappointment, love, and even hate. Grateful, there is a biblical passage Romans 8:28, it says, "Every single thing that you've been through is working together for your good because you love God". The word is UNBUNTU. There is no real English translation, but in its purest form it means "I am because you are". Today say to someone, something, some situation, "Thank you for being in my life, because it's working for you". #Ubuntu

Be Inspired!

SENSORY PERCEPTION

When we are faced with difficult circumstances and situations how do we handle them? Often times, my initial response has been to look at these times based on my sensory perception. You might ask what is that? The senses are sight, touch, hearing, taste, and smell. We tend to base most of our decisions on these factors. The only thing about this method is that sometimes the senses can be misleading. You've all heard the expression, "It's not the way it looks, or it's not as bad as it sounds, or even that taste just like chicken". Recently I was confronted with a difficult choice that I had to make that concerns my health. I'll be honest, I know God on a personal level but that wasn't my first response. I first looked at the situation and circumstances, then I looked to God. Even Jesus when faced with the cross experience asked if there was another way initially or take this cup from me. (Luke 22:42), but then the spirit kicked in and He said, "But not my will but yours be done". God has shown up in our lives in so many different ways. He has never failed, been wrong, or late. So, I say to my bad news, "God your will be done". And I hear Him saying, "I got this too". I will trust in the Lord.

Be Inspired!

NEWS, NEWS & MORE NEWS

News, news, and more news. There is fake news, good news, and bad news. We are inundated with so much news. Always someone talking to us, telling us what they want us to know. Everything is vying for space in your head. God uses this same medium to talk to you, your head. The enemy uses your head as well. There's a biblical account found in Numbers 13: 27-33 about people seeing the same thing and reporting different news. The question comes to this, whose report will you believe? I suggest that in order to answer this question you have to be spiritually awake, fit to see that all the information/news that we are being given is to alter your perception, and we know that your perceptions are your realities. If you are not listening to the report of God, you might just be getting some fake trumped up news (no pun intended). God's news is good news.

Be Inspired!

EXPECT

Were you all aware that the word expect in its original form means to wait or to look out for? The word wait is a word given as a command. It is given to someone letting them know to stay in one place until another command is given. It also says that while you are in that place you are looking out for something to take place after the wait. There is a military term or command associated with the word wait. It is Mark time. When this command is given the soldier goes from a position of doing nothing to marching in place but not moving in any direction with the anticipation of moving forward. The biblical passage found in Isaiah 40:31 says, "But they that wait (they that Mark time, they obey his command, they that expect His next command while in a position of readiness) shall find new strength, be strong like eagles, have endurance, and not faint". Expect, Wait, and Look out for God's next command for your life.

Be Inspired!

JOURNEY

Boat, bicycle, car, train, and airplane are all means of transportation to move from one place to another. This is the definition of the word journey. We are always moving from one place to another in a physical sense. There then has to be another type of journey because sometimes we are not able or have the ability to physically move. Other ways we move would be mentally, emotionally, financially, and spiritually. In reality then we are always on a journey going somewhere. So, even though you might not recognize movement in your life, because it might be so small and undetectable, doesn't mean your journey has ended. Your focus then should be, "It's not about how fast or slow I'm moving, but where or what am I moving to". A couple of simple prayers to help out on your journey Ps 119:133, "God direct my footsteps according to your word", Ps 5:8, "Lead me God in the right path, make your way plain for me to follow". So that you are not led in the wrong direction and saying, "I'm lost", consult with the orchestrator and conductor for directions.

Be Inspired!

PROCESS

The process is defined as a series of actions or steps taken in order to achieve a particular end. As I go through the process of healing, I'm asked to take a series of actions that cause me pain on top of the pain that I'm already experiencing. My initial response is, "Wait a minute I can't do what you are asking of me because I'm in too much pain already". I want the reward of the process, but don't want to go through the work of the process. Once the therapist explains that it's the only way to get to a place of healing, so you have to push through this temporary uncomfortable pain and trust the process. I then said, "Let's get it"! I'm reminded of a bible passage found in Luke 22:42 where Jesus ask God if there was another way but after seeing the bigger picture, he says, "Not my will, but your will be done". Trust every step of the process, it's necessary.

Be Inspired!

AFFIRMATIONS

I am saved, I'm free, I'm delivered, I'm called, I'm chosen, I'm predestined, I'm spiritual, I'm healed, I'm commissioned, I'm redeemed, I have purpose, I walk by faith and not by sight, I have power over the enemy inside and outside of me, I'm the head and not the tail, and I'm more than a conqueror. Wait a minute all the self-acclamations and affirmations, these are things that I should be saying to and about myself every day. However, let's not get it twisted, these things are only possible because of Christ who lives in me. All of my righteousness is as filthy rags. There is a biblical passage that says, "That it's not my works that brought me out of darkness, because I would boast. It was God's amazing grace". If I dare lose sight on this, you will see the opposite of all these acclamations and affirmations. Listen to these words, don't let them depart from you.

Be Inspired!

LAUNCH FORTH

No one can tell me that my struggles were based on how strong I was. I say that because I am stronger than I was prior to those struggles. Which lets me know that the struggles I face now, however difficult they may appear, on the other side of these bad boys there is liberty, there is healing, there is deliverance, and there is strength. Luke 8:22 say, "Now it came to pass on a certain day, that he went into a ship with his disciples: and he said to them, Let us go over to the other side of the lake. And they launched forth."

(American King James Version)

Be Inspired!

POLITICALLY AWARE

I'm not usually politically correct or even politically inclined, meaning I probably won't be running for a political office. On the other hand, I do try to be politically aware. This country (USA) has a new and different president. But here is something to get excited about, if you have a relationship with God. The Bible says this about God. 1 Timothy 6 says, "God is Lord of Lords and King of Kings". Hebrews 13:8 says, "He is the same today, yesterday, and forever". Deuteronomy 31: 6 says, "God will never leave you nor forsake you". Psalms 27:1 says, "The Lord is my light and He saves me whom shall I fear". When the political system all around me is like sinking sand, I have a rock on which I can stand, Jesus, and against it the gates of hell shall not prevail.

Be Inspired!

MY SON

I made a surprise visit to see my dad. He was visibly
surprised to see me. We hugged and then we talked on
into the night. He really liked my new vehicle so, we got
up the next morning and went to breakfast. He wanted to
go to one of his favorite eateries. Some of his hang out
buddies were there. He introduced me with these words.
"This is my son Anthony and I'm very pleased with him."
After our visit was over, I was traveling home and tears
began to roll down my face for two reasons; one, for the
words he said, and two because I was thinking that I want
to hear God say those same words about me! WOW

Be Inspired!

MY FATHER DR. JAMES H. FELTUS SR.

TREES

I was looking at trees in my mind, all kinds of trees.

When God made trees, I don't believe that every step in

the process of development of the tree He had to go back

and add something else. He put everything that the tree

could ever be in the seed. That's got to be the same way

He created us. Everything we could ever be is already in

us. Genesis 1:31 says, "God said everything He made

was very good". YES, YOU CAN, YES YOU ARE,

And YES YOU WILL!

MACHINE

I can remember back when I joined the United States Navy. Two essential things they really stressed were Attention To Detail and Working Together, they incorporated these two things in everything they taught. They said, "If adhered to, we would be a lean mean unstoppable machine". A machine is defined as an apparatus using or applying mechanical power and having several parts, each with a definite function and together performing a particular task. As believers of God we are admonished to be and do the same. There is a biblical passage found in 1Peter 5:8 that says, "Be serious! Be alert!" 1Corinthians 12:27 says, "Each one of you is a part of the body of Christ." It has always been said, "Together we stand and divided we fall". Division does not equal freedom, with people it's equivalent to failure.

Be Inspired!

PRAYER

People are hurting all around us every day, all day. They are searching for solutions, answers, and a way out of what seems to be no way. Well, I believe that prayer is the answer. Prayer is defined as solemn request for help or an expression of thanks addressed to God, even an object of worship. I believe that the most powerful Prayer one can pray is LORD HELP ME. It does several things. 1. It acknowledges God as supreme. 2. It says that you are going to the ultimate fixer of any situation. 3. It puts faith into motion. 4. It gives you an expectation of a positive outcome. 5. Not only those things, but it puts on notice whatever your source of trouble, whether it be external or internal, that you have had a conversation with something greater than any trouble. You've all heard folk say, " I'm gone tell my daddy on you", that meant you are in trouble now. Life sometimes brings us to a place of real concern, but God can handle all your concerns. My Prayer today, not only for myself but for those in trouble is LORD HELP US.

Be Inspired!

DELIVERANCE

This word is from two Latin words, de or away and liberate or set free. It is the action of being rescued or set free. Many of us can identify with this word. Some try to act as if this is not a relevant word, you know the folk that act like they ain't never had no issues. Deliverance does not mean that the thing that had you in bondage is gone, and you know what that was, it means that instead of it having dominion over you, you now have dominion over it but it's still there. Every now and then it will let you know it is still there. There is a biblical passage found in Luke 22:31-32. It says that the thing that has you down will overtake you, but it won't take you out. When you get back on your feet go help someone else to get up. So, you're getting up or being delivered was predetermined or predestined for a purpose. Deliverance.

Be Inspired!

THE MOST POWERFUL NAMES

There are two names mentioned on this planet more than any other. Those names are JESUS and God. They are discussed, talked about, put down, fought over, thought about, used in negative connotations, conversations, and disputes. They are used by people that believe in them and people that don't believe in them. They are lifesaving and life changing. Demons tremble at the very sound of the name. When your situations, circumstances, and/or conditions find out that you have called these names they begin to alter their course. The Bible says that there is no name higher, or more powerful, or by which men may be saved. I know the song says call Tyrone, but you call Tyrone if you want to, I'm gone call on someone that can help this old wretched man.

Be Inspired!

ROSES

I was in conversation with a friend about roses. We weren't talking about the beautiful colors or the different types of arrangements that make a room light up when they enter. We weren't even discussing the wonderful fragrances they emit or the smiles they put on the faces of the receivers. The point I brought up about the rose was the thorny part. Here it is, the thorn is an integral part of the rose. In other words, it makes the rose whole. Chew on that for a second. The thing that stands out to me about the thorny part is if you ever get pricked or have been pricked you will realize or have realized at that moment nothing else matters more than that prick. It captures all of your attention at that moment. It brings about change, and makes you rethink how to proceed from that moment forward. There is a biblical passage found in Acts 2:37-38. It says when they heard the message, they were pricked in their ♥, and said to the messenger what must we now do? Then the messenger told them to turn away from their old ways, repent and be baptized in the name of Jesus for the forgiveness of sin, and you will receive power.

Be Inspired!

STATEMENTS

A statement in any form, whether written, pictures, signed, or verbal, is used to reach someone. It is best when that statement is uttered, to speak or communicate in the most simplistic way possible so that the receiver, whatever their level of understanding, will be able to comprehend. LISTEN! However, I have learned that there are some things, no matter how they are spoken, will not be understood. Example, there is and has been this perception of the " church", I purposely didn't say religion. Usually uttered by non-believers. There is a biblical passage found in 2Corinthians 2:14. It says, the person without the Spirit does not accept the things that come from the Spirit of God but considers them foolishness and cannot understand them because they are discerned only through the Spirit. So, understand that.

Be Inspired!

WINNING

This word is familiar to us all. Most people view this word as something that is exclusive. We look at it in terms of personal or team victory. Well I want to take another look at this word. I want to suggest the word Winning, instead of being exclusive, is all inclusive. In other words when one person wins everyone wins. When one team wins, we all win. We may not all get the money or plaque, but because we are all connected in some way, we all WIN. Let me give you a couple of examples. When the US won Olympic Gold, it affected every American. A more important win was Jesus defeated sin and death. We, as believers, have all become victorious and winners.

Be Inspired!

PROVISION

Everyone has what they have. Some have more than others based on different factors. Sometimes the factor was a personal choice made. The factor could be someone else's doing. You know what the factor is. But let's look ᗝᗣ deeper into this word. Webster talks about Provision this way, 1. the action of providing, 2. Something supplied, or 3. a set aside amount. The Latin meaning is to foresee or attend to. We usually see Provision as some type of blessing from God. Well, all that is good stuff, but there is another answer to this question of Provision. There is a biblical passage (Gen. 22:14) that mentions one of the attributes or names of God. That is Jehovah- Jireh, translated Dominus videt, or the Lord will provide. In other words, instead of the Provision coming from God He now becomes the Provision. Some might have to wait until service is over to get that. Do you want a blessing, or do you want the blesser?

Be Inspired

PASTOR JEROME CARODINE

Life has taught me that it's good to have someone or if possible, a few someone's in your life that believes in you. Not just believe in you to celebrate your victories, but also believe in you enough to set you straight when they see you off course. You have to be willing to receive both from that person. I have been fortunate to have many such people. I don't usually use names, but I will this time. Pastor Jerome Carodine. Don't know if he remembers but 20 years ago around this time, he gave me an opportunity to preach my first sermon. Title of the sermon was "A Damascus like experience". After the sermon he caught me by myself and told me the story about Elijah. When he told the people that there would be no rain for three years and he hid himself by the brook and the ravens fed him. Then Pastor stop using me. I didn't understand why. Today, I understand better why. When I thought I was ready he believed in me enough to let me know I wasn't ready. Now 20 years later I just got an invitation to be the Keynote Speaker at an event this coming Saturday. Allow someone that believes in you the room to tell you the whole truth. Thanks Pastor.

Be inspired!

PASTOR JEROME CARODINE

MY DREAM

I'm telling this dream in order to help someone along their journey. In the dream I was in a familiar place with, familiar people. There was a group of preachers that had assembled outside a residence. We were having a rally there because of the activity that was going on at the residence. After the rally we all decided to go to a church service. The preachers lined up in columns of twos and I was on the outside of the column like a cadence caller. We marched a short distance and off to the right of us we came upon a big carnival. My attention was drawn to the carnival and before I knew it the preachers kept marching straight and I turned left. When I turned left, I realized that I was walking into the carnival and as I continued to walk into the carnival, I made a series of left turns. Before I knew it, I was lost in the carnival. I then ran into people that I hadn't seen in a long time they appeared to be comfortable in the carnival, but I said I can't stay I'm going somewhere I have some place to be. At that moment I made a right turn. I walked further, I saw another guy I knew, and he said, "Come on I'm going that way", I said, "Why not maybe he knows the way out or back". We walked together for a while but got nowhere. I stopped at a corner store and asked directions, but they didn't speak English they just pointed so we walked in the direction they pointed.

The carnival got bigger as we walked. Up to this point I was just walking through the carnival. We then came

upon a game that really caught my attention and I got
involved in the game for a short time. I went from a

look   to now being caught up. I said wait a minute
I am not supposed to be here, so I walked further and
made another right turn. The guy I was with didn't play
the game, so he left me. I came upon a familiar place that
I thought would lead me back, but it was a shortcut.
It was a dark alley with lots of noises. I heard a voice say
that there are some creatures down there that won't kill
you, but they are very distracting, you have to fight
through them. As I worked my way through all the
distractions, I came upon a very big creature that was the
biggest distraction and I woke up. When I woke up from
the dream, I couldn't move it was like my mind woke up,
but my body was still there. I then shook myself and got
out of bed.
In my spirit I knew the meaning of this dream for me. I
had just seen my reality in a dream. I pray that it is
helpful to someone else.

Be Inspired!

TO BE CONTINUED

Made in the USA
Middletown, DE
05 June 2022

66566363R00102